S0-AGO-153

THE LION & THE PRINCESS

THE LION & THE PRINCESS

ESSAYS

T. SHER SINGH

MACAULIFFE
BOOKS CANADA

www.macauliffebooks.com

Copyright © Macauliffe Books Canada 2018

Macauliffe Books Canada
Website: *MacauliffeBooks.com*
Email: *MacauliffeBooks@gmail.com*

ISBN: 978-1-9994291-0-2

Images, front & back of dust jacket:
details from hand-crafted kirpans by
American master sword-maker Jot Singh Khalsa.
Courtesy – Khalsa Kirpans.

*For my dear friend
Birinder Singh Ahluwalia
for his support and guidance
through the decades*

CONTENTS

Each Sikh male has the common last name, 'Singh' – literally, Lion. Each Sikh female has been given an equal status and an identity independent of the male, her father or husband, through the common last name, 'Kaur' – literally, Princess. The Lion and the Princess designations are meant to convey the personal sovereignty of each individual and the expectation that he and she will live a life shaped by truth and integrity, and will stand-out and be out-standing in everything they do.

GROWING UP IN HIS SHADOW

None of the recent political shenanigans one hears about from the Bihar State in Eastern India have deterred me from continuing to proclaim myself a proud Bihari. How could I not? Born and brought up in the Old City of Patna in the land of Buddha and Mahavira, of Chandragupta, Ashoka and Chanakya, where Sita was born and where the heroes of the Mahabharta gambolled, I have always revelled in the moniker.

But the clincher for my ego was that I was born not far from the birthplace and neighbourhood of young Gobind Rai, the son of Tegh Bahadar who later succeeded his father as our Tenth Guru. He is the one who would become the sixth soul to take Amrit on the historic First Vaisakhi Day, and be transformed into Gobind Singh.

Once known as Pataliputra, the capital of the great Mauryan empire, it now honours Guru Gobind Singh in its new name, Patna Sahib.

It's my only claim to fame, but it is no small mercy for which I thank my Maker. Being a Bihari who spent the first 21 years of his life in the State's capital city has shaped me in so many different ways.

My childhood and early years are therefore different from those of most other Sikhs who hail from Punjab, because West Punjab (now in Pakistan, since 1947) is where my parents fled from during the great human tragedy of Partition, and East Punjab was for me but a place to visit every now and then to see relatives or to explore the part of Sikhdom that was now left to a diminished India.

My earliest memories of Patna are, of course, of the Gurdwara. Being the birthplace of Gobind, the sprawling complex constitutes a Takht, one of the four original Thrones (now five) of temporal authority in Sikhdom.

It was a much smaller edifice then. Its features remain etched in my mind since my earliest days in considerable detail even though none of the original structure, sadly, is around today. Probably because we were there so often and because I saw the old structure being taken down and the new, current one being built before my very eyes.

One of the earliest detailed accounts of Sikhs by European travelers date back to March 1, 1781, a mere four months after Ranjit Singh was born in distant Punjab. Sir Charles Wilkins, an eminent orientalist of the time, visited Patna on that day and wrote a marvellous account of it titled *"The Seeks and Their College at Patna"* which was published by *The Asiatic Society* in 1788.

I marvel at his description of the main building of the Gurdwara because it is little different from what I remember it from more than 170 years later. He writes:

"The whole building forms a square of about 40 feet, raised from the ground about six or eight steps. The hall is in the centre, divided from four other apartments by wooden arches upon pillars of the same materials, all neatly carved. The room is rather longer than it is broad. The floor was covered with a neat carpet ..."

The building he describes was burnt down in a fire in the early nineteenth century, and rebuilt by Ranjit Singh, by then the Emperor of Punjab. It must have been built along the original lines because it is a similar building I saw through my childhood.

I also remember the commotion and the massive mess and operation around the building of a grand new, monumental gurdwara beginning around the time I was barely four years old. Yes, my memory from my earliest days remains sharp. I remember the regular visits to do seva as volunteers from across the country came in droves to help in the construction.

I vividly remember the hullabaloo around the arrival of Yadvinder Singh, the then Maharaja of Patiala – the late father of Amrinder Singh, the current Chief Minister of the State. It had stirred the imagination of all Indians that a Prince would dirty his hands and soil his clothes to personally carry cement and bricks up the scaffolding. It seemed to give everyone added fervour. I remember the electricity in the air while he and his entourage did their seva mingling freely with the rest of the workers.

Once we moved to the new part of the city – Patna Junction, it is called – our visits to the Gurdwara continued but were mostly limited to Sundays. Each trip therefore was an event because it involved a full day's outing since it was a dozen miles away now and driving through the laneways of the old city which had been demarcated centuries ago required deft negotiations with pedestrians, horse carriages, rickshaws and cattle, all of whom claimed greater right of way.

Gurpurabs are Sikh high holidays marking important historical days such as the birth anniversaries of Guru Nanak and Guru Gobind Singh, the martyrdom anniversaries of Guru Arjan and Guru Tegh Bahadar, and Vaisakhi. They were always extra special and we looked forward to them all year long. The Guru Gobind Singh Gurpurab was particularly a red-letter day … three days, actually, even spilling over into a full week.

4

First of all, it meant that our uncles, aunts and cousins and friends from all over the country would turn up for several days. And they stayed with us no matter how many. Billeting merely became cosier if more turned up, but 20-30 or more guests at a time staying over was not unusual. There's a Punjabi saying: "Raise a knee, snuggle in one more Singh!"

The Gurpurab itself would be at least a full three-day affair with programs going on all day and late into each night. The excitement began in Patna Junction around the smaller local gurdwara near the railway station a few blocks away from where we lived. *Parbhat pheris* – pre-dawn processions between Sikh homes, not unlike Christmas-time carol-singing in the West, began a couple of weeks leading up to each important gurpurab. It was a blast for us kids because it always involved the culmination of the morning at some friend's home for tea and snacks.

I'd be home from boarding school for these high holidays and it would give me a chance to let my world know that I was back in town for fun and frolic. The highlights of the Gurpurab itself were many:

The *Kavi Darbar*, the Poetry Night, was one which oddly even the young ones enjoyed to the hilt. Poets, raagis, folk singers and classical musicians of the highest calibre, Sikh and non-Sikh, would turn up for it and regaled us with their latest creations. It was the only time we got to

5

hear song and music in Punjabi; they were the days even before gramophones became popular – predecessors of the later-day turn-tables and subsequent technology. Bihar being a Hindi-speaking area, there was no Punjabi to be heard anywhere on radio or otherwise.

The *jaloos*, a grand parade more than a couple of miles long and trudging through several miles of the city, would take much of a second day, cutting a swathe through the teeming populace. It was always a delight because it invariably involved, unlike its poorer counterparts in the West, exotic delights: Nihang warriors on horses or performing *gatka's* martial arts feats, richly caparisoned camels and elephants, flower bedecked wonders posing as floats, and moving concerts on trucks by the likes of Punjabi folk-singing-icons Hazara Singh Ramta, Surinder Kaur and Asa Singh Mastana.

The whole town Sikh and non-Sikh alike seemed to be there along the route.

My father's role during these days added a further dimension for us. He was always averse to accepting any position on the gurdwara committee but consistently agreed to one seva which remained his till the time we left the land for Canada. He would take on the responsibility of running the overall Langar operations. Which involved feeding well over a hundred thousand souls three meals a day. On special anniversaries such as the Guru Gobind Singh Tercentenary in 1966/67 and the Guru Nanak Quincentenary in 1969 over 300,000 entered the city for the Gurpurab and had to be fed.

Which meant that despite the wall-to-wall people I could always find him in the langar area whenever, for example, I needed urgent candy money at any time day or night over the three days. There was a downside to it as well: we, his kids, had no choice but to do langar seva for a minimum of one hour each morning and evening. It was a must. To be honest we were no volunteers because the pocket money thus earned could easily be qualified as wages.

The competing draws weren't easy to handle. My cousins would be waiting and there was always so much to catch up with and so much to do. The bazaars too were summoning us with the aroma of street food which permeated every nook and corner. There were sumptuous sights to see: jugglers, snake charmers, animal trainers, Tibetan monks down from the mountains for the winter, fascinating yoga contortionists, wierd Hindu 'holy-men' (*sadhus*). Yet, the lure of the *kirtan jathaas* remained strong. These singers of hymns were the cream of the crop and easily overwhelmed us. My cousins and I liked good kirtan and seemed to share the same favourites.

The final day and night was not to be missed, not a minute of it. Through the years Presidents, Prime Ministers, national heroes, movie stars, all would sooner or later turn up to pay their respects at the Gurdwara and to address the masses. The climax would be on the final night when the best raagis would rev up things to a crescendo inside the main hall as the focus would shift indoors for the final hours. A few thousand stalwarts would have saved places inside all day around the sanctum sanctorum marking the birthplace of Gobind Rai, to watch the climax of the service from up close. At the same time, tens of thousands participated from the pavilions outside with a large stage of their own with parallel goings-on. Around 2 am or so the culminating 'birthday service' concluded.

I can't remember a single year I lived in Patna to have missed the Gurpurab.

In the Old City of Patna, there were signs of the boy Gobind Rai everywhere. Being told the stories and taken to the very places where they had unfolded three centuries earlier was like following him through the laneways as he was growing up. I fell in love with this child so full of life and tried to imagine how it must have been for him. I knew he had learnt to speak in the local Bihari dialects because the language comes through loud and clear in its unadulterated sweetness in the verses that are identified from his pen in the *Dasam Granth* (The Book of the Tenth Guru).

This is where he played with his little friends by the well and teased the village women by aiming his catapult at their clay water-pots. That is where he pulled out his play arrows and shot at their replacement brass pots as they busied themselves in filling them up. The well is still there and so are some of the catapult clay balls and arrows on display from the period.

The mansion and estate of Raja Maini and his Rani are but a short walk away. It is where the latter watched Gobind play and pined for, in her words, 'a son like him.' They still serve *ghuggni* (black *chhole* – peas) as sacrament at the gurdwara where they had lived. It was little changed, furniture and all, from its original form when I was there last. The snack was still served there, the very same that Gobind asked her to serve every time he visited her, assuring her that if she wanted a son like him, he would be hers too.

Head the other way and you find yourself at a dock where the River Ganges used to whisper by; it doesn't any more, I'm told, because it has changed its course a bit and now rages by a mile away. It is where the boy Gobind had lobbed his gold bracelet far into the river to point out exactly where he had lost his other one the day before.

I could even imagine what he wore. I can weave my own image of him in my mind based on his ancient shirt on display at the Takht Sahib along with some other artefacts, albeit none are in a very good state, I'm afraid. All of this aroused my interest in this boy, fuelled by the biographical stories of the extraordinary Man he grew up to be from my parents and baby-sitters.

I remember that when I was but ten years old Brother Johnson in our Grade 7 class assigned us our Thursday essay topic, "The Most Unforgettable Character I've Met", pointing to the Reader's Digest series under that title but urging us to chose our own subjects. It was an easy one for me. I chose Gobind because I felt I already knew him. Indeed, by this time he was already an acquaintance, nay, a friend.

There were other forces at work too.

Patna University at this time had a strong contingent of Sikh students led by a charismatic young man, Bawa Jaswant Singh. He now headed The Patna Sikh Students' Association which had developed through the years a good reputation as a cultural and educational group led by a new post-Independence generation of go-getters.

I remember Bawa because he was a powerful orator. He had a thundering voice and an elephant's memory. Since my father was a Patron of the Association he visited us often. I'll never forget a gift he once bought me for my birthday: a BB Gun.

Well, the friendship between him and my father led to my being conscripted to give a "speech" on the life of Guru Gobind Singh every December at their annual Gurpurab celebrations which were held in the University Senate Hall and had the local literati and glitterati in full attendance. Which meant weeks of misery for a young boy not yet into his teens. It would ruin my winter holidays as I fretted over writing the speech which was part of the deal, and at the same time striving desperately, each year, to get out of it.

The day of the actual delivery each year was not a pleasant one. I would sweat all day, first in fearful anticipation, then in my uncomfortable formal school blazer and tie. For heaven's sake, these were my winter holidays! Finally my turn would come and I would somehow make my way up to the podium. To my little stature, a hall full of several hundred adults, many of them VIPs, looked like a gladiatorial arena. Yes, I had already seen the film 'Quo Vadis' a few times at school by now.

As I stood under the glare my legs would start shaking uncontrollably until they were numb and all sensation was lost. As I struggled to hide the trembling in my voice my next worry would be how was I going to get back down the stairs and back to my seat if I couldn't even feel my legs.

Within a couple of years after one such event the leading local English daily, The Indian Nation, asked me for the script. I was glad to get rid of it. The next thing I knew it was on the front page of the weekend edition. Seeing my name in newsprint for the first time was no small boost to my self-confidence but the usual trauma of public speaking remained for a long time. It would take the first two years of law school twenty years later to completely conquer the nervousness of public exposure.

11

But my career as a writer and a journalist had begun.

The research I was forced into in order to prepare for these speeches took me into the very heart of Guru Gobind Singh's life. The more I dug and found the more I liked it and the hungrier I became for more. It also began my life-long addiction to the acquisition of books.

The childish little speeches gave rise to demands for articles. Not long thereafter, S. Mohan Singh Kalra, Editor of *The Sikh Review* in Calcutta was in the audience. He urged me to send him stuff and then unleashed that tyrannical monster that I still grapple with today – the Deadline.

I was moved to distraction by his encouragement and wanted to try something unique, something different, something that would change the world for ever. I turned to the credal story of Vaisakhi. But even my tender years found it extremely limiting to write a mere regurgitated account of it.

So in my naivety I turned to fiction.

I imagined myself as Dya Ram heading into Anandpur in answer to a call from Guru Gobind Rai for a Vaisakhi gathering, and related the days that followed through his eyes. Seeing it in *The Sikh Review*, a really long and meandering 'short story', was another shot in the arm. Thus I suppose I became a writer. But strangely enough, I wouldn't tackle fiction again for another forty years or so. (I wonder why.)

Add to this entire mix the fact that Patna, being a Takht, was a magnet for the most interesting characters in the world.

We lived but a stone-throw away from the Patna Junction railway station. It was the only local stop in the region for the national trains during my early years that serviced the Old City a dozen miles away. Therefore it sometimes fell on my Dad to bring home many of the visiting VIPs for the initial tea and refreshments before driving them to the Takht Sahib. As a result, I had the pleasure of matching names with live faces, often in our own 'drawing room', long before I fully understood what they were famous or notorious for.

Master Tara Singh is the earliest one I remember. Baba Gurdit Singh of *Komagata Maru* fame was once over for dinner – it was the first time I heard of a distant and exotic land called Canada.

Giani Kartar Singh, Gian Singh Rarewala, Sirdar Kapur Singh, Partap Singh Kairon, Hukam Singh, Ujjal Singh, Fateh Singh ... Jai Prakash Narayan, Vinobha Bhave ...

My father would bore me to death before and after every such event, trying to explain who the person was, what he or she had done, their historical significance, etc. The refrain I remember most vividly is: "Son, remember, the 'great' ones are no different from you or me. Only, they believe in something, they work hard, and they forge ahead."

All of this continued with a strange twist of fate shortly after I finished high school and joined Patna University in 1965 as a Science student (it's true, it began with science.) I was informed one day as I came back from a holiday in the hills that I had been elected in absentia as the President of The Patna Sikh Students' Association. Indeed I was a university student now and qualified, but they had no idea that I was just short of 16 years old. My nascent beard and mature looks had fooled them all.

"Try it out for a bit," suggested my father when he heard that I wanted to refuse the position. What followed was an education in so many delightful and stressful ways. In short shrift, through the events and programs of a very busy and effective association I learnt the rudiments of being a small-town impresario, a speaker, a writer, an editor, a publisher …

I let my imagination fly and tried whatever and wherever it led me, subject of course to the limitations I had in time, skills and resources. I was able to bring in my favourite people from across the country to wow our members and audiences at the seminars and conferences we held. Some through quirks of destiny led to life-transforming friendships.

The famous World War I air ace Hardit Singh Malik – also a top bureaucrat, diplomat and golfer – fell ill a few days before he was due to fly in as a key-note speaker. He offered to come nevertheless when my mother promised to host him at our home and look after his health needs. Three days of face-to-face hero-worship with this Renaissance man led to a pen-friendship.

Then there was the scholar Dr. Ganda Singh who had certain dietary restrictions because of his age. He stayed with us for a few days. That too led to a long friendship and his allowing me immediately thereafter to publish one of his books, "*Sikhs & Sikhism*" – my first publishing venture – while I was still in my mid-teens.

The artist Kirpal Singh stood out because of his tip-to-toe black tunic and eccentric persona. I can't remember why but he stayed with us. Years later after we had moved to Canada I had the delight of reconnecting with him during a trip back to Chandigarh, Punjab expressly to meet up with him. He painted three masterpieces for me. One of them, at my request, was of Guru Gobind Singh in the Battle of Bhangani.

Thus in that town where I was born and where I grew up there was nothing I touched, nothing I bumped into, that didn't remind me of The Man and of how much I owed to Him.

None of all that I have described and so much more would have happened or led to any good if it hadn't been for my good fortune to be born in Gobind Rai's 'hood and to fall in love with the life and work of Guru Gobind Singh.

Six decades later, I still marvel at this extraordinary Man. I truly know of no equal in human history.

GOD THE PARTICLE

Sometimes I feel sorry for God.

Having created him in our own image we, Geppetto-like, won't let him come alive unless it is on our terms. We define him, categorize him, label him, give him age, assign him gender, paint him angry, colour him unhappy, set him on a high chair, then coddle him, praise him, encourage him, taunt him, fawn on him, sing lullabies to him ... and then put him on a dusty shelf and forget all about him for a week.

Until the next day designated for him: the following Friday or Saturday or Sunday, or whatever.

We are forever re-inventing him in our ever-shifting self-image. Our distant ancestors saw him as wind and thunder, fire and flood. Even as a giant sperm-spouting male penis. They magnified him in geometric progression until they couldn't handle him.

Then they proceeded to divide him. Surely, with all the duties we ascribed to him, he had to be a committee. With all the power we gave him he had to be cut down to size. Hence, God the Creator, God the Preserver, God the Destroyer, God the Father, God the Son.

Not enough. It did not explain everything that was happening around us despite us and inspite of us. So we added mystery. There was a part of God we couldn't understand, so all of the un-understandables were thrown together into a huge basket which was thenceforth called, for the lack of a better term, the Mystery.

The bit we thought we did understand, we then peeled it, sliced it, diced it, cubed it, chopped it, minced it, shredded it, and mashed it up into little, manageable bits. Zeus. Neptune. Thor. Saraswati. Kali. Vishkarma. Ganesh. A saint in charge of every day in the calendar. Prophets galore. A thousand Buddhas.

Whatever was left of the big God was now a grumpy one. He got upset easily: if you ate an apple against his orders, you got banished for ever. Humanity would have to pay until eternity for the indiscretion. He became not very forgiving. And very vengeful. Locusts, hellfire and brimstone became his favourite weapons. Earthquakes became commonplace. He would part seas to save the ones he liked, to drown the ones he didn't.

He became hugely egotistical. We were required to sing his glory. All the time. And build huge temples in his honour.

18

Everywhere. He was getting unmanageable. So, we turned him into an old man, gave him a big beard and a frown.

To appease him we tore around as if we are his thugs and he the godfather, beating people into submission so that they would join us in paying him homage. In the way we told them to, no other. Or else, we just killed the unbelievers. We blew them up. We gassed them. We burnt them alive. We tortured them and then starved them. We took their homes away. And their lands. And their oil.

We knew this made him happy. And in his pleasure he started sending us special envoys to act out operas, tragedies and morality plays. One special envoy, for example, would be allowed to suffer at our hands, and in return for his suffering we would all be forgiven.

Why? How? Oh, remember, it's all a mystery.

Having reduced God to our size, we began to scoff at him. Did we really need him anymore? Yes, we do. No, we don't. Thus began new battles. We broke off our link with God and latched our fate with the monkeys. We could perform our own miracles now. Who needed God anymore?

We taunted him. Said we were bigger and stronger. It produced titanic results. We created our own weaponry, this time big enough to destroy ourselves. If that isn't power what else is. We, the Destroyer.

Who needs God anymore to do it. Sure, we can't create but we sure can destroy it all. And to prove it all we went digging deep into the earth to find the key to God's power, the single source that creates all matter. If we could find it, it would be wonderful. We could not only destroy ourselves then – mankind, this earth, all creatures – but we could even threaten to turn the entire universe into a black hole.

And, guess what? We found it, we found the 'key'.

The God Particle.

God, once again, in our own image. Reduced, manageable, in our control. Now finally we have it all. The trigger is in our hand, the finger is poised over the red button.

Quickly, let's hand out the Nobels, before we get working with this, this P-A-R-T-I-C-L-E.

What can God do anymore, now that we have reduced him to a particle. We have him in our fist. Back-off ... or else.

Boy, we're so good.

God? Oh, just tell him, we're busy. Don't call us, we'll call you.

FREEDOM DON'T COME EASY

It was our third day in Fez, a medieval city in central Morocco. It was Christmas Eve. My daughter, then in her early teens, and I were on a holiday.

This morning we were back in the medina to once again explore its miles and miles of ancient bazaars and to take in its sounds, its colours, its smells. We entered from the south-eastern gate to the walled city. Gathered next to the spot where we parked our car was a crowd. Our guide explained: it was a weekly souk, a market, this one of birds.

We dove into the melee. There were birds on sale everywhere – a myriad of exotic species, as well as the run-of-the-mill, table variety. Four categories in all, our guide explained. Birds which would be cooked and eaten; song birds, bought for their melody, or plumed ones, as pets;

birds of prey such as falcons for hunting purposes; and those merely used as bait to lure other birds or animals into traps and snares.

We were saddened to see these lovely creatures crowded into terribly small cages often so cramped that they could barely move. There were hundreds of birds but virtually no chirping. As if the birds could sense that they were in dire straits.

My daughter was particularly distressed. She muttered under her breath as we struggled from one spot to another, from one cage to the next.

"How rude!" she would exclaim, over and over again. "Don't these owners have any feelings?"

At one point she leaned over and to my utter shock whispered: "I want to kick this man. How can he treat his birds like this?"

She wanted to free all the birds. So I signalled to our guide and we left very quickly. We entered the medina from the closest gate and proceeded to explore its labyrinthine laneways.

My daughter remained pensive all morning. But at one point when our guide reminded us that it was Friday – Jumma, the Muslim Sabbath – and the markets would all close for the day at 1 pm, she seemed to have arrived at a decision. She announced that she wanted to return to the bird market. She wanted to buy a bird and set it free.

Why, I asked.

"I want to free them all. Their faces haunt me. If I can't afford to do that, I'll buy one and make it free."

We had barely forty minutes left, so we ran all the way back to the ancient walled gate. Once we got there we made a bee-line for a cluster of cages in the thick of the chaos and zeroed in on a stack of doves piled atop each other in layers in one of them.

It took her an age to choose the one she wanted to buy; they all looked so much in need of freedom. Finally, a sad looking one was selected. Spotlessly white. She paid. The vendor pulled it out of its cage. Its wings were scotch-taped down to prevent it from flying. Before we could say a word, he began to rip the tape off. The dove screeched as its feathers were torn from its wings.

My daughter snatched the bird from him, giving him a scowl. We fled to the fringe of the crowd. She carefully took off the rest of the tape. She comforted the bird and gently stroked its feathers back into place.

By this time we had attracted some attention. Word had got around that a bird was going to be set free. Dozens followed us wherever we went, many coaxing us to give it to them.

She was oblivious to them all. She walked to the edge of the plateau and, facing the descending slope of the valley below, set the dove free by propelling it into the air.

The poor bird floundered and in seconds was back on the ground only a few feet away, unable to take off again. Then all hell broke loose.

A dozen figures immediately pounced on the bird. The bird hopped around a bit. They fumbled around in a storm of dust. One of them got it. Another snatched it from him. He, the victor – a twenty-year-old or so – emerged with the bird held high. He sneered at us and waved it back and forth in triumph.

Now what do we do, I muttered to myself. I didn't have time to answer.

The next thing I knew my fifteen-year-old daughter dived onto him, threw him to the ground, pushed him, shoved him, grabbed him, shook him, pelted him ... until he let the bird go.

She had it back in her hand. In an instant, she was back on her feet. She launched the terrified creature again into the air. "Fly! Fly!" she screamed after it.

The bird faltered. And then somehow sensed it was now or never. It suddenly seemed to regain strength and to remember that it had to spread out its wings and flap them. It did a perfect arc into the air. Flew around us once and then disappeared into the valley below.

There was pin-drop silence for a few seconds.

I stood there stunned, gearing up for a riot. The urchins were frozen in motion, assessing the situation, I'm sure.

My daughter beamed from ear to ear. "Yes! Yes! Yes!" was all she could say.

The other fellow was now back on his feet. He taunted us from a safe distance: "You Arabi! You, you Sahara!" he yelled, as if in insult.

Moroccans, you see, had considerable difficulty figuring out my turban and our nationality.

"Non," a voice from the French-speaking crowd corrected him, "Indien."

My daughter swung around, the triumphant smile still on her face. Her expression seemed to read: You misjudged this one too, buddy.

But all she said was: "N-o-n. Je suis Sikh – et Canadien!"

No, I'm a Sikh … and a Canadian.

"Aa-ahh," responded the crowd, almost in chorus, as if that explained it all.

My *sher-di-bacchi* dusted her coat. She had lived up to the sobriquet we often teased her with: the progeny of a lion.

I stared at her for a long moment. I recognized in her something that had always been there, except I hadn't noticed it before. I smiled. We walked away.

THE VISIT

A repeated tap on the metal bed-post woke me up. I would've faded back to sleep but an even louder rattle inches from my ear jolted me to a sitting position. I looked around. It was still dark, the dormitory's rows of white beds barely discernible. I was groggy and unable to focus on any explanation when I heard a familiar gruff voice behind me. I swung around, tangling myself in the sheet I'd been lying under. It was Brother Bosco towering over me.

"Come on, Singh, get up," he was trying to whisper but his deep voice did not allow much muffling.

I noted with relief even through the haze of sleep that he'd called me "Singh" and not "Baby Singh", the nickname I had acquired the previous year in Brother Carr's Grade Six, being by far the youngest kid in the class. Having graduated to the Senior Dormitory must've helped, though at 11 years of age I was still the youngest in the hall.

27

The boys in nearby beds had started stirring. "Go back to sleep, all of you," Br. Bosco hissed and then turned to me again. "Come on, come on, let's go."

I slid off the bed and by force of habit began to do the bed, pulling up the counterpane.

"No, no," Br. Bosco shouted. "Leave it. Let's go … now!"

He marched off manoeuvring his way around the beds, shushing and scolding as other heads were raised curious at the commotion. I stumbled along sliding in and out of my slippers as I tried to keep pace with him, too out of it to even wonder why. As we passed the corridor leading to the dormitory washrooms I glanced at the clock overhead.

Four o'clock, it read, with the minute hand barely past the first quarter.

"Get out of your pyjamas, quickly," Br. Bosco barked at me, his voice back to normal.

We were in the box-room which is what we called the hall with the rows of cupboards that held all our worldly belongings. Big George, the one-eyed giant caretaker whose job it was to keep the hundred and more young boys in this Senior dormitory on constant military ship-shape, was standing in the shadows. He had his usual cane in his hand. He pointed to a cupboard, guessing I couldn't see too clearly in the dark.

As I passed him I noticed he had a patch over his right eye. I made a mental note, a juicy tid-bit to be shared with my friends later: that he took his glass-eye out at night.

He switched on his flash-light and guided me to my cupboard. I fumbled with the lock and key, the latter hanging by a string around my neck.

"Dress up quickly, Singh. In any shirt and pants. Doesn't matter what ..."

Br. Bosco hovered in the shadows. That meant I was safe: George wouldn't – couldn't – whip a kid in sight of a Brother.

I had begun to wonder what was happening but didn't dare ask. You didn't ask questions; you simply did what you were told to do. That was the rule, especially if the instructions were coming from a teacher or staff. We marched down the stairs in a procession, Br. Bosco leading, George and I behind him, and then our three resident Boxers and the lone Alsatian merrily wagging behind us.

The corridors downstairs were lit but there was no one else in sight. We walked to the edge of the verandah and Br Bosco pointed towards the darkness beyond. I stared. I couldn't see anything. I looked up at him.

"Go ahead, go ahead, they're waiting for you," he said gruffly and jabbed a finger into me.

I jumped down to the ground and began walking towards where I knew there was a copse of mango trees filling up the space between the red school-chapel on the left and the school's front portico and main office on the right. I could see that a light was on in the parlour where visitors were

29

usually received by the Principal. I began to walk towards the distant light but stopped when I heard voices from the direction of the trees.

I looked more intently and made out the silhouette of a car and a couple of figures standing next to it.

"Tapesh!" I heard a voice call me. There was only one person in the world who called me that: Brother Burke, our Principal. "Here. This way. Come here, young man!" His Irish accent was unmistakable.

I approached them. Out of the shadows materialized the apparition of Br. Burke. Next to him stood my father. Behind them was our family car, the loyal Austin A-40.

I froze. An 11-year old's mind can conjure up a bundle of fantasies each more nightmarish than the other, in a split second. They flooded my brain as I tried to make sense of the scene. I looked back: Br. Bosco and George were still standing on the verandah. The dogs had hopped down with me and had encircled me, wondering, I suppose, if they should bark but seemed to be comforted by Br. Burke's presence. They simply whimpered and crowded around me, tentatively flicking their behinds.

I looked back at the duo in front of me. My father had his arms out-stretched. I ran into his embrace.

"I'll be in the office, Ishar. Let me know when you're done," said Br. Burke, as he walked away.

"Am I going home?" I asked.

My father simply smothered me and laughed.

"Is it Sunday?" I asked, freeing myself finally. I searched his face. He looked different. It had a glow to it. And his beard was open, flowing down to his chest. I had never seen him in public like this. At home, yes, but outdoors, it was always neatly rolled and dressed.

I looked into the car. A lone male figure sat in the passenger seat. A male. A Sardar. "Is it Sunday?" I mumbled again. "Where's Biji?"

Sundays were the regular visit days when the whole family – Pita ji, Biji, my sisters Davinder and Sunder, and my brother Artaj, by now a few months old, would all turn up at my school. It was usually in the evening when the rest of the boarders were in study mode. My mother would unravel my hair, then still in a French braid, as was common with many young Sikh boys then. And she would wash it under the taps right beside the hand-ball courts, then dry it, comb it, oil it (yechh!) and braid it back … prim and shiny, good for another week.

"No, it isn't Sunday," said my father, smiling. "That's Sardar Kirpal Singh in the car … go ahead, wish him Sat Sri Akal."

I joined my hands and lifted them in the air in greeting towards the shadow in the car.

"But why did you come this early? It's four in the morning!" I whispered, part embarrassed, part alarmed.

31

"I'm off to Delhi. I wanted to stop on the way and tell you I'll be gone for a bit and to say good bye." He pulled me towards him and put his arms around me again.

I shook myself free. "But why?"

He reached into the car and pulled out a bag. "Here. Your mother's sent you some things."

"But why are you going alone? Where's Biji? And the shop – who'll look after it while you're gone?" It just didn't make sense.

He leaned against the car, pulling me close to him. "I'm going to Delhi alone. Your mother is staying behind. Bhajan, your cousin who's been itching to learn the trade and claims he knows the ropes by now, will look after the business while I'm gone. It could be a few weeks before I'll be back. Maybe more."

"You're going for business?" I asked. And then added: "But you never go so far by car on business. How long for?" Delhi, I knew, was roughly a thousand miles away. That is, at least two or three days' journey in those days.

He shook his head. "No, it isn't for business. I'm going to help some people."

"Doing what?" I shrilled.

"There's a lot happening in Delhi and Punjab. A *morcha* … you know, a struggle. The community has risen, united …"

"A what? I don't understand, Dad! A struggle? Will there be trouble? Are you going to be in danger? Is that why you're going in the night? Are you in trouble?"

32

"No," he smiled, and then turned sombre. "This trip was put together in a hurry, in a few hours actually. I have to drive because I'm carrying a lot of cash. It's safer this way. I need to go to a number of different cities. It'll be a long journey, so we've decided to start early. It'll still take us a few days. Kirpal Singh ji is coming with me to help in the driving so that we don't have to linger along the way."

"What's happening, Dad? You're not telling me everything. Tell me the truth ...!" Tears welled up, cracking my raised voice.

He was silent for a while. Then continued.

"Sikhs in Punjab are fighting for 'Punjabi Suba' ..."

"Fighting? You said it was safe? I don't understand ..."

He motioned me to be patient and began to explain. It was mostly mumbo-jumbo to me. Sikhs were asking that their state, Punjab, be like the rest of the country. With a language of its own. So that it was truly a Punjabi language state and the language could be protected. So that we could all learn to speak and write and read Punjabi. Punjabi Suba meant a Punjabi-speaking region. Otherwise, the language would die. And that couldn't be allowed to happen because if it did, our cultural heritage would die, our community would suffer.

"Don't worry, beta. It's a fight but a non-violent one. All that our people are doing is courting arrest by the thousands. The government doesn't want them to protest and

33

has declared a curfew everywhere. Still, they're coming out in waves, overwhelming the government which still refuses to listen to them. All the Sikhs want is what the other communities in the country already have."

"But this sounds dangerous, Dad. Will they put you in jail?"

He laughed. "No, they won't put me in jail. I'm not going to be out there protesting. That's not what I'm going for. My job is easy."

"How long will this last? How long will you be away?"

"I don't know because I have to do a lot of traveling. But who knows? The jails in Delhi and Punjab, in fact all over, are already full. There's no more room, so many keep on coming. They're shipping off the newly arrested protesters now in trains to jails in other parts of the country. So I don't know how long. There are already two hundred thousand and more behind bars. Men, women and children, they keep on coming."

His explanation didn't help. It made me all the more panicky.

"Tell me truthfully ... are you going to be jailed?" I asked, my eyes flooded.

"I don't think so," he said. "I'm on a different mission. Many of the people jailed are bread-winners. With them locked up, their families need help to survive. So Sikhs all over are collecting funds to help support their families to feed them, to pay their rent, while they're spending time in prison. We want to honour their sacrifices."

"But why do you have to go to Delhi?" I demanded.

"The Sikhs in Patna got together and have collected a lot of money. They've asked me to take the cash and deliver it into the right hands. So, my job is to deliver the money to the communities in Delhi, Amritsar and other cities in Punjab."

"But why you? Why not someone else?" I implored.

He explained that he had volunteered because one of my *maasis* – mother's sisters – had courted arrest. She had recently given birth but when she heard that they were running out of men and needed women to continue the struggle, she insisted on joining the *morcha*. So she too was in jail but with her two-month-old daughter.

"I need to get baby-food and medicines to her somehow. If she can do this for the common cause I want to do my share though it isn't much. I have the easy part. All I have to do is bribe some people and get the stuff in and make sure it gets to her. And others like her."

"What if they lock you up too," I moaned.

"They won't. My mission is different. I promise I'll be careful."

He drew me closer and comforted me.

"I wanted to see you before I headed out so that you know what's happening. You are the man of the house now.

Make sure you're strong. And when you see your mother, be her strength."

"Will I be going home, then," I asked, suddenly excited by the prospect.

He shook his head. I was to stay in school but my mother would continue visiting me every Sunday. He had arranged for our neighbours, the Bedis, to bring her to visit me.

They couldn't stay long, he said. He walked me to the Principal's office. It was still dark though there was promise of light on the horizon.

I felt Br Burke's hand gently rest on my shoulders as he stood with me on the portico. The Austin drove away, the lights slowly receding up the long driveway. It hesitated for a moment at the gate, which I knew from memory carried the inscription emblazoned on its inside: "Quis ut Deus?" – "Who is like God?"

The car turned right and immediately disappeared behind the wall that ran along the school boundary, heading northwards toward Delhi.

Jail. Fight. Struggle. Sacrifice. I had never heard these words in this way. They didn't make sense. All I knew was that my father had appeared mysteriously in the middle of the night and then a few minutes later disappeared into the darkness. I wasn't quite sure why. To do what. Where. How …

I suddenly felt, for the first time in my young life, the weight of the world on my shoulders.

WHAT'S WITH THIS UNITY THING ANYWAY?

What's with this 'unity' thing? Everywhere I turn the excuse Sikhs give for their failures and shortcomings is the lament that we are not united.

"If only we were united …" It's a blanket justification used by many to hide personal laziness both intellectual and physical. And cover their cowardice or incompetence or just a basic lack of passion, commitment or even talent and skills.

Unity? You think Christians, the largest religious grouping in the world today, are united? The other day I came across a document, produced by a Christian Church which cites 41,000 Christian denominations that exist today. That's the exact number they have come up with through their own research. "If only we were united …," they cry.

Jews? There appear to be as many Jewish groups as there are individuals in the community, many within the community will tell you. Those on one end of the spectrum won't even speak to those at the other. Some would rather kill the others than be caught dead in the same room with them.

Muslims? It began with Sunni and Shia. Now you have a thousand splinters.

Buddhists? Have you ever been to South-East Asia? There's a whole world of variations ... more shades of saffron than you can imagine.

Hindus? Well, each of the billion of them seems to have a very personal deity, some of them not even dead yet. They worship everything under the sun ... including the sun. Each has a personal animal, vermin, plant, rock, planet or politician to worship. The only thing that appears to unite them all, if you look at Hindutva's India today, is greed.

Sikhs? I don't know, but I keep on coming across people from every faith imaginable who tell me: "If only we were as united as the Sikhs we could ..."

The first time this happened was when I was about 10 years old, and it was the Hindu editor of The Indian Nation newspaper saying that to me in Patna ... yes, to a 10-year-old. The last time I heard it said in identical terms was from a Jewish Rabbi in Toronto not too long ago. The world sees us as united, stuck together like glue. We are universally envied for this unity. We are resented for this very unity.

They look at our small numbers and they take note of how we have as many as 14 gurdwaras in Toronto alone, for example. And each is attended by thousands every Sunday. On every week-day evening too. Across the road Christian churches belonging to the majority religion of the land get visits from a few dozen each for an hour on Sunday mornings and then the buildings stay neatly locked up for the rest of the week.

Each member of the Sikh congregations seems to be gainfully employed. All look far more affluent than the national average. Everyone marvels at how we fight for our rights relentlessly ... until we win.

There's never been a time I can remember when some nitwit somewhere didn't come up with, "No, you can't wear a turban here, because ... you know, because, well, because we never have ..." Or one of a dozen variations of this remarkable observation.

Each time we have won even if it meant going all the way to the Supreme Court. Even while our billion detractors in India beat themselves in a frenzy, crying, "No, don't, no, don't, they are violent people!" we have used due process, democratic and legal avenues, and never violence, more efficiently than anyone else around. And we've always won. Even if it took years and millions of dollars for each struggle. Even when the power of the state opposed us, or the weight of the mob.

"If only we were as united as you are ...," they tell me.

They can't figure out how we dare to wear our turban crowns in every land, on every street, in every corridor of power and influence, and do it with a smile and a swagger while Christians hide their crosses under their shirts when it becomes unfashionable or inconvenient to do so. Hindu Brahmin males have chopped off their mandatory 'shikhas' (pigtail-like tufts of hair) until you can't find one in sight anymore in much of India. Jews hide their names and their yarmulkes when identity does not work in their favour.

But Sikhs ... well, Sikhs do turban-tying demonstrations out in the open, in public squares. And competitions where Sikh mothers of little children undeterred by hate crimes bring them in and demand that they be taught to tie a dastaar like a prince. Truly, in this day and age I've seen nothing braver and daring than such mothers of tender-age boys.

So, what's this unity thing that everyone keeps clamouring about?

Are you united within your family at home? Do each one of you see eye to eye? Do all of your friends and loved ones even vote for the same political party? Do you know of any group that does?

I thought one of the strengths of our community is that we have leaders and followers of every political persuasion. As a community we are not a monolith, thank God. After all, we are encouraged to think for ourselves. Being human, not lemmings, we have divergences of opinion. Vive la difference!

So, does that make us not united? I think unity as envisaged in a thoughtless way is, like peace, a pipe dream. It ain't gonna happen. Not the way most people think of it. Not here, nor there. Not with us, nor with any other grouping within the homo sapiens.

But I know what you want and what you're looking for. And THAT is going to happen not by muttering over and over again, "Let's have Unity!", but by getting off our butts and doing what we would like others to do. You think we should make an epic movie on Ranjit Singh? Put a bundle of money on the table – any amount, even $10,000, if you can't afford more – and see how it multiplies. Add the yeast of personal action and by the next morning it'll be a loaf of bread a hundred times the original size.

You want to counter the propaganda spewed out by goons hired by India's corrupt politicians? Put your money where your mouth is. You lament the loss of our heritage and culture? Start supporting Sikh writers, playwrights, dancers, filmmakers, journalists, TV & radio programmes. You are being discriminated at work? Help build our advocacy institutions.

That is what unity is about. It's not a train that will choo-choo into town one day and bring in the militia. Unity is within each one of us to discover. Once we unite the *miri* and *piri* within ourselves, all other unity will follow.

Next time you're looking for unity outside you and around you, remember, unity is not a first step or a tool ... it is an end product. And, it begins with YOU and ME.

PRIDE AND PREJUDICE

We were on a cruise in the Caribbean. As the ship sailed out of Santo Domingo's harbour the first afternoon we were apprised of details of our itinerary as well as the protocol to be followed while on board. The ship would be out in the sea each night sailing to the next port of call. It would arrive there in the early hours and we would have all day to explore the island on our own. We were free to stay on board to enjoy its facilities but if we went on shore we were to be back no later than the assigned time, shortly after which the ship would head out once again to the next destination.

Dinner every night was to be a formal affair. One could opt out of formal dining and eat in one of the many restaurants and cafes that were sprinkled around the floating city. We opted for fine dining which meant we had to rest, wash up and get ready within a couple of hours after we were back on board each evening. Business suit and tie and evening dress were the minimum requirements for entry into the dining hall. Four couples were assigned to each dining table and we would be the same dinner companions every night for the entire voyage.

The first night went off well. My friend and I introduced ourselves to the other six at our table. The couple to our left was a honeymooning couple from Toronto – her third marriage, his second. Joannie Squires was chipper as a songbird and never let things get dull at our table. Steve, a pleasant chap, deferred to her and followed her lead.

The couple to our right were from Mont-Joli in Quebec: Gils Martin, a gentleman farmer, Marie, a farm-wife. They spoke English reasonably well but Joannie who had been brought up in Montreal often engaged them in French. The bilingual element added a nice dimension to our lengthy evenings together.

While the six of us were in the range of 45 to 55 the couple across from us was certainly older. They were more reserved but polite and courteous at all times. They said very little either on our first night or on any of the nights that followed. "Jim" and "Hilary Davidson" their table name-tags revealed. "From Kitchener, Ontario" was all that Hilary volunteered when one of us pressed for more information.

That got me digging for more since Kitchener was but 30 minutes from where we lived. "Retired" is all that I could get out of her. He merely smiled or nodded or shrugged in answer.

The days that followed were perfect. In Guadeloupe we shared a day-long rental car with the Squires and pottered around in the countryside. We got together again to do the same in Antigua to uncover its colonial history. In Sint Maarten the Squires and the Martins joined us, first for lunch and a stroll through the shopping district and then for a lazy afternoon on the beach.

However, no matter how hard we tried we couldn't lure the Davidsons into joining us ashore even once. In fact we realized before long that they never left the ship. They just weren't social. To each his own, we muttered to each other. We did persist for the first few nights in trying to draw the Davidsons into our dinner banter but they proved as tough as nails. He would mumble a few inaudible words around a smile. Or she would offer a short answer and then they'd clam up.

My friend and I spoke about it amongst ourselves a few times. Both of us knew the type well: the reserved, aloof air of those who still carried baggage from their British origins. We recognized it as the sad remnant of a colonial mentality. Both of us in our respective experiences had learned to live with such an attitude by showing it indifference. Once we had pigeon-holed it we filed away our diagnosis in our minds and didn't talk much about it anymore.

At dinner the Davidsons remained aloof but polite and we humoured them. We managed to pass our time through the voyage without an untoward incident or an unkind word. After all we were all on vacation and each of us seemed to be adept at not letting anything dampen our spirits.

The days flew by. Seven islands and seven days later we were back in Santo Domingo. It was time to disembark and be driven to the airport and be flown home to Canada. The exodus was well organized. There were several exit points on the ship. My friend and I were in line awaiting our turn to get into an elevator which would then disgorge us onto a gangplank which would then deliver us to the waiting buses.

We hung around patiently as did all in our line; a second, parallel queue beside us wound its way to a second elevator. As I glanced around my eyes caught those of Hilary Davidson standing beside her husband. She nodded and smiled. I smiled back. Jim turned and looked at me and smiled. I reciprocated.

My friend and I turned to each other and blinked a silent and resigned "Whatever!" to each other.

I felt a tap on my shoulder. It was Hilary. Jim was straggling behind her.

"Can we have a word with you?" she said softly.

"Sure," I said.

"Can we sit down somewhere, please? Jim wants to say something. It'll take only a minute. But somewhere quiet ..."

We had time. We pulled out of the queue and retreated to the other end of the floor where we found a cluster of sofas. Jim touched my arm and gently motioned me to sit down next to him. Hilary sat on the next chair. I turned to him; he was looking down at the floor as if struggling with his thoughts.

"Yes?" I was getting impatient. It must have shown in my voice.

Hilary leant over, and said, "Jim wants to say something, and he wants to say it himself."

I stared at her. "Sorry, Sher," she continued, "Jim suffered a stroke a few months ago and therefore can't speak easily. So, he'll be slow. Just give him a bit ..."

I looked at Jim. He looked at me and smiled. And nodded. And then slowly, syllable by syllable, word by word, he whispered:

"I follow your weekly columns in The Record. I am a big fan of your writing. I just wanted to say, 'Thank You!' "

It seemed to drain him.

Hilary interjected: "He has his favourite columns by you stuck up on the fridge. And he mails them to our daughter in Winnipeg to read. He's been wanting to say this to you all week, but you know this stroke has left him helpless. He can't carry on a conversation any more. I am hoping this week in warm weather will help."

As we said our goodbyes I didn't say much. I stayed seated on the sofa after they left. I asked my friend to go with them. I said I'll follow in a moment.

I sat there for a long time, staring at the sea. A steward finally came and said that I had to go or I'd miss the bus.

NEITHER A SHIELD, NOR A SWORD

I have noticed that the concept of *seva* – loosely translated as "selfless, voluntary service" – is nowadays increasingly wielded as a weapon and less as what it is meant to be.

The other day when a community volunteer was asked why she repeatedly failed to do what she had undertaken to do, why she hadn't met her obligations fully or in a timely fashion, I was flabbergasted by the response I overheard:

"I do seva, bhen ji", she protested. "I'm not getting paid for this. I spend so many hours here while I could easily be doing something else. I don't have to listen to this nonsense: if you don't want me here, say so, and I'm gone!"

It was a deft use of the very essence of seva. As a shield – a shield from criticism and from accountability.

On another occasion, I heard a fellow wield the word

somewhat differently, but equally effectively. He was addressing members of a community group.

"I'm the one who can run this organization and ensure that it stays alive. I've done seva for three years day and night and weekends too. And haven't taken a single cent for my time. How can you even think that another person should come over and run it? Others will simply run it to the ground. And you know I'm not going to let you do this. I'm not going to let you turn all my seva into nought."

I felt as I watched him through this performance that he was wielding his seva quite deftly ... as a weapon. A sword, actually. The parry and thrust was working: you could see it in the wounded look in the eyes of the audience.

Is this what seva is all about? Am I wrong in thinking that the moment you use seva ... yes, U-S-E it ... for any ulterior purpose, then it instantly ceases to be seva? If it loses its spiritual core, then all you're left with is a clumsy weapon.

The concept of seva is simple and uncomplicated in Sikhi. The very idea of seva begins with a metaphor: that of the milk-pot or vessel. Nanak says:

First, wash the vessel,
Next, disinfect it with incense.
Then, and only then, is it ready to receive the milk.

–GGS, M1, 728:1

50

True. What good is the milk once it has been poured into a soiled receptacle? The dirt of the vessel taints everything that is poured into it. The mind like the vessel first needs to be cleansed if one is to prepare it for things spiritual. Otherwise all effort goes to waste. And this cleansing of the mind, the preparation, is done with the 'soap' of humility.

So far all of this is esoteric and philosophical. But Sikhi brings the exercise down to earth by guiding us how to do it while going about our day-to-day ordinary lives. In seeking humility there's no need to blindly wade through religious tomes. No penances, no fasting, no retreats, no masochism of any kind. No feeding of priests, no pilgrimages, no ritual baths, no renunciations, no onerous abstentions.

There's a simple, direct and effective way: seva.

No grandiose projects are necessary for this inner cleansing. We don't have to build monuments or light bonfires on top of mountains or even go on far-flung crusades fighting for world peace. Just serving the basic needs of those who are in need puts us on the right path. At home, with the neighbour, around the corner, in the community we live in … the concentric circles can get as wide or remain as narrow as the situation demands.

Feed the hungry, clothe the destitute, shelter the homeless. Or even more simply: just wash the dishes at the langar hall or serve food or look after the shoes of those who come to worship.

Anonymity helps. Not wearing a t-shirt or bandana that proclaims SEVADAAR, helps. Doing it without fan-fare, without a shabaash or pat on the back, is a definite plus. Doing things that others do not want to, or cannot do, is good. Sweeping the floor or cleaning the washrooms are therefore bound to be the most rewarding.

One of the most moving sights I have seen in my life is something I witnessed a few years ago in Espanola, New Mexico. Singh Sahib Harbhajan Singh Yogi had shed his mortal coil and crowds from around the globe had arrived to celebrate his life. By the thousands. The logistics required to cater to the needs of these visitors from far and wide were stupendous. And one of them was the need for a platoon of portable toilets which were, I'm sure, leased for the occasion. It would've been terribly easy to have also bought the services of a handful of workers who could've maintained the facilities and kept them clean at all times.

What touched me deep inside was the vision of our hosts who saw it as an unprecedented opportunity to do seva. Any time of the day or night if you walked into the facilities you saw a couple of the Sikhs from the Espanola sangat cleaning the toilets and water basins, or down on their hands and knees cleaning the floor. It was arguably the cleanest spot within the acreage roped in for the events of the week.

And, you know, there was not a sign anywhere proclaiming: "Seva provided by the Sangat of ..."

Nothing. Not a word, not a peep.

That's seva.

It's for the sheer sake of seva. It has no other goal. Even the end result is not important. You don't need a smile or a nod, a pat on the shoulder, or the gratitude of another to validate it. You simply do it and you do it to the best of your ability, nothing else matters. You don't go home and note it in your diary. Or tell your family and friends. Or have it published in a newsletter in the "Acknowledgment" section. And you don't wave it in the face if you are running for election the next time around.

Here's what I've been taught and what I try to emulate, though those who know me well could easily cite many a lapse:

- Don't let the right hand know what the left hand does.
- It isn't seva if it is for the purpose of getting a tax-deductible receipt.
- It isn't seva if your heart and soul aren't in it.
- It isn't seva if it isn't done with honesty and integrity.
- It isn't seva if you believe that mediocrity is all that is expected of you and that you needn't do more.
- It isn't seva if it's for building your resume.
- It isn't seva if it is meant to be a stepping stone to bigger and better things.
- It isn't seva if you need to tell others, now or later, that you did it.

- It isn't seva if lack of appreciation by others, or their criticism, drives you away.
- It isn't seva if you believe that it is your right to do it.
- It isn't seva if you have to fight against others to do it.
- It isn't seva if you snatch it away from another to do it.
- It isn't seva if you begin to believe you're the best one to do it.
- And it isn't seva if it distresses you that others take credit for what you've done.

Not too long ago I was blessed with an opportunity to visit the Golden Temple (Darbar Sahib, the holiest of holies in Sikhdom) in Amritsar, Punjab, after an absence of more than three decades.

There were so many things that added to the joy of being there. Not the least of it was the timeless sight at all hours of the day or night, literally – even in the cold and dark hours before dawn – of men, women and children behind the counter at any one of the many entrances, tending to the shoes of pilgrims. Quiet faces, moving in the shadows. Ever-so-slight, barely discernible quivering of the lips, silently accompanying the kirtan playing from the speakers around them. No small-talk. No name-tags. No meeting of the eyes, no searching for acquaintances. Just simple, purposeful, swift, efficient movements … the queues were long.

There's always a hush around the shoe-stalls particularly outside the main entrance, I've noticed. The only words you hear are "satnaam, satnaam ..." and "waheguru, waheguru ..." And a lot of "ji ... ji ... jee-o ... ji ..."

I don't know how they do it. But I see them taking each pair of foot-wear as if it is a house-warming gift. Lovingly, gently, softly. If you glance back for a split-second as you turn away, you may even catch one in the shadows carefully wiping the dirt off your shoes as they are placed on the shelves.

I tell you, it is there, standing on the cold wet marble, looking at this scene, that I experienced the first communion with what I had come searching for after all these years at the doors of the Harmandar.

It is the epitome of seva.

And, it is most magical when – and I borrow from the English Bard's 'The Merchant of Venice' – it "is not strain'd"...

It droppeth as the gentle rain from heaven
Upon the place beneath.
It is twice blest:
It blesseth him that gives and him that takes.

May we all, each one of us, be blessed with this gift.

TRAMECKSAN AND SLAMECKSAN

Several summers ago I found myself on the Stoney Indian Reserve in Nakoda which is in the middle of nowhere amidst the Rocky mountains of Alberta, Canada. I was there along with forty-five other Canadians on a week-long retreat entitled "Conversations on Canada". We had been selected from across Canada to participate in this exercise to canvass issues pertaining to Canadian identity and nationhood. All our deliberations, formal and casual, were to be recorded by two crews from the Canadian Broadcasting Corporation (CBC), one for TV and the other for radio. They would shadow us everywhere during all our waking hours to save it all for posterity.

Our host, Chief Snow of the Stoney tribe, a First Nations community, announced over our first dinner together that a brief spiritual ceremony would be held outdoors, conducted by the tribe's medicine man to seek inspiration for our deliberations. Four persons were randomly selected to symbolically represent the group in the ceremony. I happened to be one of them.

The entire crowd emerged from the lodge and gathered on the grass outside. It was still daylight. It felt like we were in Eden. The crystal-clear lake. Towering mountains all around us, still snow-capped from the previous winter. The sky vied with the lake in producing different hues of blue and green.

The Chief and the medicine man asked the four of us to follow them into a tepee standing a few feet from the water. There was no room for more inside, so the rest stood outside encircling the tepee.

Inside we sat in a circle, cross-legged on the ground. The medicine man began a chant. The Chief whispered a running translation for our benefit. The medicine man first lighted some sweet-grass. He retrieved the components of a pipe from a bag. He took out tobacco – I recognized the smell immediately – from a pouch and sprinkled some of it on the smouldering sweet-grass. He then began to fill the bowl of the pipe with the tobacco.

The Chief whispered that once the pipe was lit it would be passed around to each one of us to share. We watched all of this in fascination. My mind, however, was elsewhere galloping at a hundred miles an hour desperately looking for some quick answers.

You see, Sikhism has very few rules or do's and don't's. One is clear and unequivocal: tobacco for all Sikhs is taboo. There are no if's and but's: a Sikh is never to use tobacco in any form, for any reason. I quickly reminded myself that I had to that day never even touched a cigarette box leave alone a cigarette or any form of tobacco – yes, even touched – in my entire life. Or a pipe. Or a hookah or a hubble-bubble. Of course, I had never smoked any either.

And here I was a few seconds away from being handed a pipe. In a religious ceremony. With cameras and microphones recording every word, every move. For posterity, and to be broadcast nation-wide at some point.

There was no time to explain. Who could I talk to? The Chief was busy whispering a translation. The medicine man was chanting. The other three were understandably mesmerized. And here I was at the opening ceremony of this week-long conference symbolically representing the entire group with the media as an all-pervading witness. Was I going to let everybody down by precipitating an incident?

But then could I compromise my deeply held religious beliefs? Could a life-time of discipline be discarded on a moment's notice? How would I face my daughter the next time we discussed smoking?

But who would care anyway? In seven days all of us would part company and go our different ways and, who knows, probably never see each other again. And the other three sitting beside me would be smoking it anyway.

But then, how would I face myself in the mirror that night?

I just didn't know what to do. Certainly I did not want to offend or insult our hosts. I fully realized that tobacco had spiritual significance within Native beliefs, albeit in complete juxtaposition to the Sikh belief. I respected their belief unequivocally. And I respected mine.

The medicine man lighted the pipe. Once it was ready he drew hard on it; his eyes were closed in meditation. I could see it was like a sacrament. He then held it out, the stem in one hand, the shank in the other, and the Chief took it from him. He smoked a few puffs from it and passed it to my neighbour.

She took a whiff and turned to me.

Instinctively I leaned back a bit, put my right hand on my heart and slowly, respectfully, gestured with my left hand that it be given directly to the next person.

She did so without missing a beat as if we had rehearsed it a dozen times. I looked up and searched for clues on the faces of the Chief and the medicine man. Both smiled gently and nodded their heads.

That's it. The crisis was over. When I explained my dilemma to the Chief and the medicine man later that night over the camp-fire, they appreciated what I had done.

It wasn't an earth-shaking decision but it was one of the toughest personal decisions I have had to make in a long time. I often think of that evening, especially when I read of 'religious' strife everywhere.

The clash between my belief and the Native one on the use of tobacco, idealogically, is total. And there is no dearth of examples where each one of us believes in things which others oppose vehemently. But what is sad is that people are killed, neighbourhoods destroyed, communities wiped out, all for religious 'disputes' of far less significance.

I shudder to think what may have happened if something similar to my Nakoda incident had happened in, say, India. Or Bosnia. Germany. Ireland. Even some parts of the U.S.

Not infrequently, I also think of Gulliver and his travels in Lilliput. You will recall that he recorded stories of "two struggling parties" going under the names of Tramecksan and Slamecksan. One believed in wearing only high heels on their shoes; the other was adamant that low heels were the 'right' way.

"The animosities between these two parties run so high that they will neither eat, nor drink, nor talk with each other."

Gulliver also describes the perennial wars between the Big Endians and the Small Endians. The Big Endians supported the "primitive mode of breaking eggs", that is, from the larger end of the shell. But the Small Endians unfortunately insisted that *their* way was the Chosen Way.

There isn't a single religious war, conflict, dispute or argument anywhere in the world today – and there are so many of them – which is over anything of greater profundity than the issues that divided the Lilliputians.

The creator of Gulliver and Lilliput, Jonathan Swift, was also the Dean of St. Patrick's Cathedral in Dublin, Ireland. You should read some of his opinions on us human beings as a race.

THROWING A LION TO THE CHRISTIANS

When I was a young boy my parents sent me to a boarding school run by Irish Christian Brothers a few miles outside our city in India. I was sent there even though I was a Sikh and not a Christian, because it was reputed to provide a good education.

I was about 11 years old when during mid-school-year I had a bit of a windfall. It was the time of the year when the Catholic kids in the middle school participated in a retreat, and we, the non-Catholics, got a 10-day holiday as a result. So I arrived home one day mid-week and announced I had a holiday for ten days.

"What's the holiday for," asked my father, puzzled by my unexpected arrival.

"Oh, the Christians are having a retreat. So, I'm home," I explained, with muted glee.

Though it was a Catholic school, at that point we simply knew them as Christians. It wasn't until I arrived in Canada as a 21-year old that I discovered that the Christian world was divided between, inter alia, the Catholics and the Protestants, and that the twain did not easily meet.

Still puzzled, my father pressed on: "What's a retreat?"

I explained it's a time for prayer and meditation for the Christians. They read the Bible, the Brothers and Priests talk to them about religious matters, the kids listen and think about various matters, question a bit, spend a lot of time on their own, contemplating, reading, studying, learning, finding out about their religion.

"Hm-mm-m. So? What's Christian about that?" asked my father.

I shrugged my shoulders. Wasn't it obvious, I thought.

"Why can't you participate in this retreat?" he asked. "They pray, you pray; they meditate, you meditate; they think, you think; they contemplate, you contemplate. What's Christian about that? You listen to them, listen to their prayers and discourses; but only you can decide what goes on in your head. Right?"

Within minutes, to my utter consternation, I was shipped back to school. That year and every year after that until I completed high school I lost this precious 'holiday'. I had to participate in the retreat.

I've often thought of that first time when I felt traumatized by my father's stance. Since I am, like all other male Sikhs, a Singh – a lion – it is the only instance I know of when a lion was thrown to the Christians! A complete reversal of roles from the biblical story of Daniel that was oft heard in school during those very days.

I've often wondered what must have gone on in my father's mind when he shipped me back to school that day, straight into a Christian den, knowing full well that I would be vulnerable and exposed for ten full days with no protection, no refuge. Surely he must have worried about how my own beliefs would fare when confronted with those of another religion. Surely he must have worried about proselytizing, about my being swamped by numbers or overwhelmed by arguments. Yet he threw me right into their midst.

I spent eight years in that school. And, you know, not once, not for a moment did I ever consider changing my religion as an option. I grew up proud of my own religion, my own traditions and beliefs; but more importantly, I grew up understanding Christianity and appreciating it. I learned as a result how to look at my own faith from the outside in, and thus to be a better Sikh by being respectful of the beliefs of others.

I believe it gave me the very template of how to approach other religions, any religion, all religions. In fact I believe that I grew up directly as a result of that stance taken by my father in asking "What's Christian about that?" with the intrinsic belief that if I truly strive to be a good Sikh, I cannot help but be a Christian. And a Jew, a Muslim, a Hindu …

The opposite I believe applies too: if one is a true Christian one cannot but also be a Sikh, and of course a Jew, a Muslim, a Hindu, and a Buddhist at the same time. And so on and so forth.

But what would have happened if my father had said to me: "Good. You are right. You should not be participating in this retreat business. You are a Sikh, they are Christians. Be careful of them."

It's this 'us-and-them' business that complicates our lives and warps perfectly normal people and their perfectly normal, healthy, wholesome values out of shape and beyond all recognition.

In my situation, my father's willingness to be open and the willingness to take a risk, the willingness to teach, the willingness to learn, were the crucial ingredients. No small credit should go to the good Irish Christian Brothers either: after all, they were willing to have me hang around in their midst when they could very easily have said no.

The willingness to ignore the demarcation line between us and them at a crucial point helped to erase that line forever for me that day. I believe I'm all the richer for it.

All because a young lion was thrown one day half a century ago right into a Christian den.

THE REFUGEE

Jesus is returning to earth shortly, a news-flash proclaimed the other day. "There's a 99-per-cent probability," said Rev. Audie Derryberry of Downey Bible Church (Reformed) in California.

I remember another good soul, Harold Camping, also from sunny California, who made similar calculations and had confirmed the prognostication. He was the acknowledged expert in the field, having predicted the end of the world several times.

Well, if it is true we've got to do something about it. We've got to get a message somehow to Jesus and tell him that this just isn't the right time. He's got to be stopped, his return has got to be delayed. We need time to clean up a few things at least temporarily before he arrives. We simply cannot let him see the mess we're in.

And remember, before he even gets here he'll have to go through the refugee and immigration check-points. That's not good. They'll take one look at him, and …

His long hair and beard: they'll be unshorn and black. His tan, a dark and shiny bronze. His accent, thick and heavy, definitely Middle-Eastern. Religion? He'll have to answer "Jew" because he would never have heard the word "Christian" before.

It's summer. If I remember his garb correctly from my readings from biblical scholars, his head will be covered with a loose turban. He'll be wearing a sacky garment, an *abaaya* or a *jalabiya* robe maybe. He'll probably be bare-footed unless the road is very hot or he's planning a long trek, in which case I expect he'll be wearing hippie sandals.

He certainly won't speak, understand, read or write English (or French or Spanish). I won't be surprised if he chooses to respond in Aramaic or Arabic. Lord, the officials will hear loud alarm bells clang between their ears.

His passport stampings and ancestry will look awfully suspicious. It'll be obvious he's been wandering all over the Middle-East criss-crossing borders with unusual frequency. A refugee? A terrorist? He'll need at the very least a special permit to get in.

But, but once he's in – if he's allowed in – what will we do? What will we say to him? What will he say?

I have consulted with a fundamentalist Christian friend of mine. Who else would I go to if I wanted expert advice on Christ? He believes the first thing Christ will say when he arrives is: "Christians only, please. I'll meet with no one except Christians. Period."

Hm-mm-mn. Well, let's assume that my friend is right. In fact, that makes the itinerary easy. And the guest lists too. We will not repeat Queen Elizabeth's mistake on her recent visit to Canada: this time around no Sikhs will be invited to tea.

While mapping out his tour, we know Jesus used to like going to synagogues. But my friend tells me Jesus is now a Christian: of the Christians, by the Christians, for the Christians. So I guess no more synagogues. He'll want to visit Christian churches only.

But wait a sec! Which denominations then? Who will he want to associate with: Protestants or Catholics? Certainly not both, I bet you. Or do you think he'll limit himself to the evangelists? Billy Graham and his buddies, maybe – after all, he's a friend of Presidents.

What are his other preferences? Should he be allowed to mingle with the Mexicans, especially the "illegal aliens"? The Blacks in Harlem? The First Nations on the reservations? They're all Christians, after all, but will they pass muster?

But let's agree on one thing: let's not say a word about Abu Ghraib or Guantanamo, right? Let's stay mum about the plight of the Palestinians. We don't want to upset him.

He'll have a lot of questions. What should we tell him, and what should we hold back? The abominations of some

Jews and Muslims in the Middle-East; by the Hindus, Muslims, Sikhs and Buddhists on the Indian sub-continent? Rwanda, Somalia, Bosnia, Cambodia, Iraq, Afghanistan, Punjab (1947, 1984), the French head-covering ban, etc. – they'll all be easy to talk about because none of the victims were Christians. There's no risk it will upset him hearing about them. After all, they, the victims, have no hope in hell of getting into the Kingdom of God anyway.

But, how much do we tell him about Ireland? Do we tell him that both sides have been killing each other? In his name! Or what happened in Nazi Germany? Or the steady decimation of our aboriginal peoples the world over? After they were converted to Christianity! Do we mention the role of Christians in the colonies, the empires, the Raj, the World Wars? Korea. Vietnam. South Africa. Bosnia. Rwanda. Iraq. Afghanistan.

Let's be careful. Let's think this one out. But *before* we let him in. I'm a bit worried he might decide to get crucified all over again once he finds out all that's happened since he was here last. He'll want to wash away our sins ...

Moreover, I'm afraid that this time around we need so much absolution that just one crucifixion may not suffice. Now that I think of it, the events unleashed by his second coming may start a trend. What if Nanak, Buddha, Mohammed, Krishna and Moses also decide to return?

I tell you, it could get awfully embarrassing. For all of us. He's got to be stopped at the border.

MY HERO

I adored my father when I was a child. I thought he was strong, wise, and an infinite source of information. I hero-worshipped him and could never get enough of his time and attention.

This never changed through my teens as I developed the arrogance of the all-knowing son who, as he grew even older, just couldn't figure out how Dad had survived in this world on his own. Not unlike how my own daughter feels about me today.

My love and respect for my father survived all our inter-generational conflicts. And there were many, all the way to the day he passed away, two and a half decades ago. It is the way of the world and how the baton is passed on from one generation to another.

But I can picture the day I saw my Dad at his very best, as if it was only yesterday. The incident has stayed with me and shaped me. I see it as clear as day every time I find myself with my back against the wall and it inspires me all over again.

I was still in my pre-teens. I was home for the holidays from boarding school and liked to hang around in my father's business premises, especially when it was busy, for I enjoyed his inter-action with his customers.

"M.I.T. Motors", as his business was known, was named after my mother, Mahinder Kaur; my father, Ishar Singh; and I, his eldest son, Tapishar – the 'T' in my *nom de plume*. It was an auto-parts retail and wholesale establishment with tires as its main focus.

It was a tall building on one of the main thoroughfares of the new part of the ancient city, several stories high. The lower two floors were occupied by the business while the next two floors constituted our residence.

Patna, being the capital, was the State's seat of government. It was where my newly-married parents had fled a thousand miles away from the home they lost during the cataclysmic Partition of Punjab in 1947. The State of Bihar though rich in natural resources was then and still is known as a poor, ill-run and unruly province, plagued by a caste-ridden society, corruption and rogue politicians. Being a backwater, it was a great place for me to grow up but it did have an air of the Wild-West to it. It still does, if you think of former Chief Minister Lallu Prasad, for example.

Bihar's recent politician-scoundrel has cultivated world-wide notoriety as a buffoon in order to distract attention from the billions he has stolen from the exchequer. If you are looking for an antecedent of Canada's Ford brothers or America's Donald Trump, look no further.

Well, I grew up there and learnt the ropes in that milieu.

One morning, as I played on a type-writer beside my father in his store, three cars pulled up to a screeching halt outside, spilling a dozen white-khadi-clad men through the huge doors. 'Khaadi' is home-spun cotton made famous by Mohandas Gandhi during the Independence movement and since then worn by Indian politicians to feign their dedication to India's poor.

One of them came inside and approaching my father announced softly that "Minister Sahib", the province's Minister of Education, "would like to come in and pay his respects."

My father greeted the dignitary and welcomed him into the inside office. The Minister and his assistant sat down across the desk from my father. I remained in the office lurking behind my father's chair as I always did when there was something interesting going on. The rest of the contingent, obviously hangers-on who usually accompanied local politicians, stayed outside to light their *beedies* (local cigarettes) since smoking was strictly prohibited on the premises.

My father was well known and respected in the city, including the political establishment. The Chief Minister (it was long before the Lallu Prasad era) was a friend and the visitor appeared to be aware of this as well as of my father's general reputation. Dad was, inter alia, President of one of the local Rotary Club chapters, and chaired the city's tire industry and auto-parts dealers' association.

Tea was ordered for the entire entourage and small-talk lasted until the last drop. As a by-the-by, the Minister asked if the store had any tires in stock for his cars. Parked outside, each of the three vehicles was an Ambassador, the car-brand then favoured by the Indian politicians because they could easily squeeze-in well over a dozen men into each.

Car tires were then in dire shortage and sold at a high premium because demand far outstripped supply. My Dad said he'd be glad to be of service. "How many do you need?"

"Twelve, Ishwar Babu! All of our cars need new ones."

Knowing that the Minister was a powerful man, my father – Sardar Ishar Singh, but "Ishwar Babu" or "Sardar ji" to the Biharis – simply said: "No problem!" and turned to a servant and asked him to bring them out.

Twelve tires were rolled out. The Minister's assistant checked the size and the make, sought and received assurances that they were right and the best, and asked the servants to load them in the cars. Four were stuffed into the trunk of each car.

My father asked a store clerk to prepare a bill and added for the benefit of both the clerk and the Minister that the price charged would be the recommended list price. Which at the time was roughly half the market price. When the bill was brought in, my father respectfully offered it to the Minister's assistant who without even glancing at it folded it and put it away in his shirt pocket. The Minister and the assistant stood up. The former announced: "Good. Thank you, Sardar ji. The money will be sent to you in due time," and turned towards the door.

My father stopped him: "Sorry, Minister Sahib, but we do not give credit. Ever." And he pointed to a sign above his head which glared, in large red letters over a white background: "NO SMOKING NO CREDIT NO HIGGLING" (sic).

He looked the assistant straight in the eye and added: "We'll have to be paid in cash before the tires can be taken away."

The Minister turned around and sat down. "Ishwar Babu, you know who I am. There's nothing to worry. You'll be paid. You see, I don't carry around so much money on me."

My Dad was polite but firm: "I understand, Minister Sahib. But we have a strict policy and simply cannot make any exceptions. We'll take the tires out of the vehicles now and your assistant can come back in an hour or whatever, pay the invoice and pick up the tires. We'll have the tires put aside for you, not to worry."

The Minister was getting a bit agitated and raised his voice. "You don't trust me? You can't take my word? Don't you know who I am?"

I snuggled closer to my father's chair. I could sense that things were taking a turn for the worse.

"No, Minister Sahib. Most respectfully, we just don't do business this way. Your assistant knows this, he's been here before. The whole town knows about it. We're quite firm about it. It has nothing to do with you personally, Sir. I have the utmost regard for you. But the tires must stay here until they are fully paid for."

The Minister stood up. The others had come into the store and were now crowded around the door. His voice was raised and had begun to splutter.

"No one is going to remove those tires from my cars, do you understand? You Punjabis! You dare to come to live in my land, do business here, and then show me such disrespect. How dare you. I will simply not allow it!" He huffed and puffed, shuffling from one foot to another.

My father repeated his pleas but they were drowned by the muttering from a dozen different directions. A couple of more men had entered the office and were towering over my father who continued to sit behind his desk. I looked at him while snuggling even closer to him, alarmed by the raised voices. My father was quiet as he softly patted me on my arm. He looked at the Minister and those behind him. They scowled back.

Seconds passed, but felt like eons. Then slowly, he got out of his chair and said: "Please wait a minute. I'll be back …" He turned to me and said, "Wait here, beta, I'll be back in two minutes."

And he went out. I could hear his footsteps on the stairs and the receding echoes told me that he was going upstairs to our apartments.

The crowd grumbled, with the word "Punjabi" thrown around liberally. I didn't understand the stand-off but knew that they appeared agitated. And I knew that my father had seemed deep in thought, as if trying to make a decision.

Minutes went by. I slid into my father's chair. They glared at me as if it was all my fault. I trembled and looked away. Finally, I heard the footsteps heavily echoing down the stairwell at the back: my Dad was rearing down the stairs as he usually did in the morning, full of energy. He reappeared at the door. The crowd parted. He entered. I vacated his chair. He sat down.

He looked at the Minister who was standing with the rest of them by the door, as if chomping to leave.

My father then reached into his inside coat-pocket. As he pulled his hand out, it was almost wide open but appeared to be covering something. He placed the hand slowly, gently, palm down on the glass table-top right in front him. There was a slight metallic sound. He lifted his hand and slid it off the table.

"Okay, now, where were we?" he said softly. He was breathing a bit harder. From the four flights of stairs?

Everyone stared at the object before him.

I instantly knew what it was. He had shown it to me once before when he had first received a license to own it and had purchased it from Calcutta. A Baby Browning pistol, glistening menacingly in shades of grey. Pointed to the side, towards the wall.

"As I was saying, Minister Sahib. We'll keep the tires here, reserved and secured for you. They can be picked up as soon as the payment is brought in." And he turned around and yelled instructions to the servants: "Remove all the tires from the car-trunks and put them aside for the Minister Sahib. Now!"

The servants swivelled into action. The crowd in my father's office remained frozen. Speechless. All of them had their eyes glued on the pistol.

I remember clutching my Dad's arm and whispering "D-a-d!" He put his arm around me and pulled me closer.

It took the Minister an eternity to give a voice to his moving lips. "This is not good. You will hear from us later, Sardar ji. This is not the end of it."

He pushed through the crowd and stomped out in a huff. The rest followed. They passed our servants on the way to the cars as they rolled the tires in multiples of four back into the shop. The cars drove away in a tornado of smoke and dust.

No one said a word, neither my Dad, nor the staff. Nor I. For a long time. Everyone pretended to be busy.

But I was afraid the posse would be back before long. Should I flee upstairs or stay by my father's side?

"D-a-d?"

"Yes, beta!"

"Will they come back?"

"I don't think so. Not today."

"But why did you bring out the pistol?"

"I'm not sure, beta."

"What do you mean? Would you have used it?"

"I don't know … no, I don't think so."

"What do you mean? Then, why did you bring it?

"I don't know …"

He looked at me and comforted me by holding me close.

"What did they want, then?"

"They did not want to pay. That's all. Because they are corrupt politicians and they think they can get away with this sort of thing."

"But he said he would send you the money?"

"Yes, he did. But I don't think he ever would have. This is how they oppress people, these bad politicians."

"Are we in trouble now?"

"I don't think so. I don't know for sure, but I don't think so."

"How do you know?"

"Because such people are cowards. They take advantage of weak people. And they are afraid of those who fight back."

"But, but, why did you bring the pistol?"

He was thoughtful for a minute or two. And then broke the silence.

"I had to show them I was not afraid of them."

"You weren't afraid?"

"I think I was. But you should never let the other person know you're afraid. Because if you do, then they'll walk all over you."

"But you could have let them take the tires. They would have sent the money. He said so."

"No, he wouldn't have. If I went to the police for help they wouldn't do anything. That man has power over them. And then, whenever he would need anything from us he would send a bunch of his people and they would similarly take things from us and never pay. Because then he would know I can't do anything. Word would go out and others would try the same thing. We would be at their mercy because we would be scared. So I had no choice. I had to do what I did."

It took me years, no, decades, to fully understand what he had done. But ever since, whenever I see a show-down between cowboys in a Western, I see him standing beside Gary Cooper and Alan Ladd, Glen Ford and Audie Murphy, under the high-noon sun. Unhappy, but determined. Unwavering. Unflinching.

He'll always be my hero.

P.S. The posse? We never saw or heard from them ever again.

THE MOTH AND THE FLAME

Around June ever year when it is in the thick of the searing hot *looh* season on the Subcontinent, Sikhdom celebrates the extraordinary man who gave Sikhi two of its greatest gifts: its Scripture, known as the Guru Granth, and its central shrine, the Golden Temple.

He was in the prime of his life, a mere 39 years old, when his spiritual activities were deemed a threat to institutionalized religion by the Mughal ruler of the land. Refusing to waver from his faith, he was tortured until his body succumbed.

His name is Arjan, the Fifth Sikh Guru (Teacher). The year was 1606. It is on his shoulders on which stands much of Sikhi as we know it today.

So how do Sikhs commemorate his martyrdom? Well, here's what we've never done and still don't do:

We don't beat our breasts. We don't wear hair shirts. We don't mourn. We don't lament. We don't rail against the forces of evil and brandish recriminations. We've never been bitter.

But here's what we indeed do. It's simple.

In every city, town and village, in every neighbourhood where Sikhs live in large numbers, here's what we do to mark the day: we take some water. We add milk to it. And sugar. We then add *gulab jal* (rose-water) to give it flavour. We add chunks of ice to chill the beverage.

Then, on the day marking the great martyrdom – invariably when temperatures simmer and bake in the Celsius high 40s and sometimes even higher – we set up stalls outside our homes and businesses, on the side-walk, at street-corners. *Chhabeels* is what these shacks or tents are called, where we serve the refreshing libation to all passers-by. Free.

Nay, many do better. Volunteers spill into the streets and gently stop the traffic and offer the *kacchi lassi* (the refreshing concoction I've just described to you) to those in cars and buses, rickshaws and tuk-tuks, and ask for and accept nothing in return.

It brings no medals. No awards. No certificates. No media coverage. It's done for the sheer joy of it all. Year after year. Century after century.

This is how we celebrate – yeah, CELEBRATE – the great sacrifice. It is simple. It captures everything that Sikhi

84

offers. There is no greater glory. This is how we remember this Ideal Person who did so much that we enjoy and treasure today.

Arjan was born at Goindval, Punjab in 1563 to Bhai Jetha (who later came to be known as Guru Ram Das, the fourth Sikh Teacher) and Bibi Bhani. Though the 'baby' of the family, he was deeply spiritual. Impressed by his true piety, his father named him his successor as the next Guru; he took the mantle at the young age of 18, when the former shed his mortal coil.

Guru Arjan was a walking institution. In the ensuing 23 years of his life, he led the still-nascent community – the spark had been lit by Nanak, the founder, who was born only a century earlier, in 1469 – into maturity. He began and completed the construction of the Golden Temple in the middle of the tank in which it sits today. At the commencement of the project, he did something revolutionary: he asked Sayeen Mian Meer, a respected Sufi from Lahore – a man of a different faith – to lay the cornerstone of the new structure.

Arjan also started and took to fruition the monumental task of compiling the authentic compositions of the preceding Gurus and 15 poet-mystics (belonging to a variety of faith traditions) whose spirituality was in consonance with that of the Gurus. The investiture of the new Granth (scripture) in the new structure took place in 1604. A learned centenarian, Baba Buddha (not to be confused with the founder of Buddhism), became the first steward.

Arjan was a poet, a linguist, and a musician par excellence. He combined his talents not only in compiling the baani, but ultimately became its biggest contributor through as many as two thousand verses, which now comprise one-third of the Guru Granth. He sang:

As long as man divides his world
  into friends and enemies,
He'll remain separated from God;
As long as man discriminates
  between himself and others,
There'll remain a distance between him and God!

Not only his own compositions but also all the poetry he collected, garnered and compiled are arranged according to *raags* – musical scales constructed around content, tone and mood in Sikh and other subcontinental classical traditions. Each verse comes with a recommended *raag* and is meant to be sung, accompanied by musical instruments. Hence, Sikh scripture is intricately tied to music and poetry.

Arjan came to be known as Saccha Padshah, the True King, to his contemporaries. Which did not go well with the Mughal Emperor, Jahangir, and the Muslim clerics that surrounded him.

Jahangir wrote in his *Tuzk*: "So many of the simple-minded Hindus, nay, many foolish Muslims too, have been fascinated by the Guru's ways and teaching. For many years, the thought had been presenting itself to my mind that either I should put an end to this false traffic, or he be brought into the fold of Islam."

Ultimately, Jahangir had Arjan taken prisoner and presented with the choice in Lahore. He was tortured over the course of several days with hot plates, burning sand and boiling water. A Hindu official, Chandu, encouraged the Mughal. On the other hand, Sayeen Mian Mir, the Sufi Saint of Lahore, offered to intervene. The Guru declined his help.

With "Sweet is Thy Will, O Lord ..." on his lips, he was taken to the River Ravi nearby.

"A dip in the river's cold water was more than the blistered body could bear," writes historian Gurbachan Singh Talib. "Wrapped in meditation, the Guru peacefully passed away."

A Jesuit, Father Jerome Xavier, who witnessed all these goings-on, in a letter he wrote from Lahore on September 25, 1606, says: "In that way their good Pope died, overwhelmed by the sufferings, torments, and dishonours."

Bhai Gurdas, the great poet, scribe and chronicler of Sikhi, described it thus:

As fishes are at one with the waves of the river,
So was the Guru, immersed in the River of the Lord:
As the moth submits itself to the flame,
So was the Guru's light merged with the Divine.

In the extreme hours of suffering,
Aware was he of nothing but the Word Divine,
Like the deer who hears no sound
But the ringing of the hunter's bell.

Like the humming-bee who is wrapped in the lotus,
He passed the night of his life in a casket of bliss;
Never did he forget to utter the Lord's Word,
Even as the chatrik bird never fails to utter his song.

To the man of God,
* joy is the fruit of devotion and meditation*
With equanimity in holy company.
May I be a sacrifice unto this Guru Arjan!

THE POWER OF ONE

I recall a fable told us by my father from his recollection of a Grade Three Persian Reader.

A pious old man was riding through a forest when he heard cries of help from deep within the woods. He followed the groans until he came upon a young man lying on the ground, apparently injured and in dire pain.

"I've been robbed and beaten," he pleaded. "Help me … please don't leave me here to die!"

The rider was moved by the appeals and descended from his horse, leaving his satchels on it. He then helped the man in distress to his feet and assisted him in mounting the horse. He comforted and reassured him:

"I'll take you to the next village where you'll get balm for your wounds. Why don't you ride the horse since you're unable to walk, and I will walk beside you till we get there."

But the moment the young man was secure in the saddle he snatched the reins and burst out laughing.

"Fooled you, didn't I? Have a pleasant walk home," he taunted the baffled old man and began to gallop away.

"Stop! Wait!" yelled the old man, realizing he had been tricked. "I must tell you something before you go ... It's important!"

The thief reined in the horse, turned it around and waited at a safe distance.

"Say what you have to say quickly because I'm in a hurry."

"Well," said the old man, "you're clever and you've cheated me. You have taken advantage of my compassion and kindness. I can live with the loss of the horse and my property; I'll even give you my promise never to report you or pursue you to recover any of the things. You can keep them. They're yours now. But on one condition, though: you must promise that you will never tell anyone how you tricked me, how you took the horse from me."

"Why, fool? How does that help you?" queried the thief.

"Simple. If people ever find out how you took my things, of how I responded to your pleas for help with compassion and as a result lost all my worldly belongings, they will stop helping strangers. The wise and the wary will then counsel everybody never to be kind to strangers. I'd rather willingly give you my horse and everything I own than have you kill kindness and compassion for all time to come. So please, please don't tell anyone about you have done."

The thief, the story goes, was moved to shame by this. He returned the horse and belongings to the pious man, begged his forgiveness and promised to turn his life around.

This story has been replayed in our midst in real life.

In fact we were told this fable in the early 1970s when my father was troubled by the fact that an increasing number of incidents of abuse of/by hitch-hikers in North America was generating a new wisdom: that one should never stop for hitch-hikers.

My father caused us untold distress when he resisted our entreaties to stop giving rides to strangers. He was in the habit of stopping for hitch-hikers, or for those waiting at bus-stops on very cold, Canadian wintry days or hot and humid summer afternoons, offering free rides. They saw his Santa Claus beard and welcomed the succour.

He would cut through our scolding and dismiss us summarily: "You can't let a few criminals change our quality of life."

DAILY COMMUNION

My dear friend, Inni Kaur, lost her mother to an illness a few summers ago. Years later she still feels as if it was yesterday.

"I miss her terribly," she says. "The intense pain has now become a dull ache. My mornings are the hardest. She lived in New Delhi, India, I here in Connecticut, USA. But, she was part of my daily routine. Every morning after I listened to the *hukam* from the Golden Temple via my computer I would call her on the phone. It would be around 6 pm her time ..."

Hukam?

Literally the word means a royal edict or command. It refers to the first verse read out from the Golden Temple each day, chosen that morning by the reader in the sanctum sanctorum of the holiest of holies in Sikhdom by opening the Sikh Scripture at random.

Consisting of spiritual and mystical poetry, the verse

provides a thought or two to meditate on for the day to all those who hear it that morning.

"The first thing we would discuss during the telephone call would be the morning's hukam," Inni reminisces. "She would've heard it several hours earlier at 4 am her time, simultaneous to its reading which she would catch on the live broadcast on the TV or radio. She would make a conscious effort to study the passage some time during the day knowing that I would call. And we would then discuss it before moving on to other things."

Listening to or following the 'hukam' from the Golden Temple is not religiously mandated. It is neither a ritual nor does it carry any spiritual brownie points. Especially since the hukams are read separately, each one invariably being different, in millions of homes and gurdwaras around the world.

Why? It's like a spiritual Thought of the Day. It is meditative and it is meant to inspire, to provoke introspection. The process encourages contemplation and hopefully keeps the individual mindful of one's spiritual role in life as one goes about the day's worldly chores.

Nothing detracts from those who don't or can't tune into the one read out from the Golden Temple; the ones chosen at random in each of the households scattered around the world serve the purpose equally.

"At times," explains Inni talking about the daily conversations she used to have with her Mom, "I would say to her:

'Ma, listening to today's hukam, I feel the Lord is pulling my ears.' She would laugh and reply, 'Inni, if He does not pull your ears, who will? You aren't one to allow anyone else to pull your ears?'

"Point taken, Mother."

It is exactly such personal exchanges between people or individual introspections that are hopefully triggered amongst the 30 million Sikhs who live in Punjab, in the U.S., Canada, Europe and elsewhere in the diaspora and 'take/receive' a hukam that day.

In gurdwaras located in large Sikh communities, especially where daily services are held, a scholar may provide an interpretation or discourse on the concepts covered by the day's hukam selected at that gurdwara. Or the one from the Golden Temple in Amritsar. Though the page opened at random may vary from place to place, home to home, what makes this exercise universal and unites the community worldwide is that the actual scripture referred to is exactly the same everywhere.

It is the Guru Granth which is treated like a living teacher in the sense of The Living Word, but to the nth degree. It is the sole and ultimate spiritual guide to a faith which tolerates no human spiritual leadership, not even a priesthood. The language and script; the number of pages (1430); the format, layout and pagination; the punctuation – every element is exactly the same, unaltered everywhere. No translations or exegeses are used for this purpose.

That is, no matter who opens a copy of the Guru Granth, anywhere – in the Golden Temple in Amritsar, or in my humble home here in Mount Forest, Ontario, Canada, or any other place in between – it is exactly the same text with no difference whatsoever in its content. The idea is that each Sikh must seek his or her own meaning and apply it to his or her life to the best of his or her wisdom.

But what makes the daily exchange with her mother that Inni describes and now misses so poignantly special, is the miracle of modern technology that we have been blessed with incrementally within the current generations, especially in my lifetime. Not too long ago, within living memory, only those who could be present within the precincts of the Golden Temple complex could hear the actual voice reading the daily hukam live and contemporaneously. Those curious as to the exact verse selected in the Golden Temple that day could only pick up the citation in a newspaper, for example, the next day. The rest of the Sikh world merely sought guidance from their own personal hukams 'received' in their own local spheres, respectively.

Then came the radio. Which widened the concentric circle. And then television and live broadcasts across Punjab and other parts of the subcontinent.

From that point on, the changes have been in leaps and bounds, and now tentacle around the world. Computers and cable, satellite relays, laptops, iPhones and iPads, cus-tom-made ringtones, texting and apps – each development seems to add a new dimension, new possibilities, quick, nay, instant access. You can be in a speeding car on a remote highway or flying in a jet over the ocean, if you are even slightly more tech-savvy than I am you can hear or even see a simulcast. Or access it later from your own gadget of choice at your leisure.

This is the marriage of natural evolution and man-made modernity at its best. The forces of cyberspace have come together at their own pace almost on their own will to bring us together as a single, united community every day and at every moment of each day, to listen to the mag-ical sounds and words of song and poetry emanating from Amritsar.

It is all the more a miracle in that it is not a requirement to tune in. It has never been recommended anywhere, never mandated or made a prerequisite to any activity, nor does it promise any rewards. Those who are pulled by it have surrendered to it voluntarily and willingly.

The morning hukam from the Golden Temple taken recently, for example, was as follows. I offer you a loose English translation. Not an ideal or perfect one, it carries none of the magic of the original words or the timbre of the singer. But it serves the purpose nevertheless.

I am satisfied and satiated
Eating the food of truth.
With my mind, body and tongue
I meditate on the Lord.
Life, spiritual life, is in the Lord,
Consisting of singing His Name
In the company of the pious.
He who sings His praises
Finds himself in raiments rich,
He rides elephants, chariots and horses,
If he finds His path in his own heart.
Meditating at His feet,
Deep within mind and body,
Nanak has found the Lord,
The treasure of peace.

—COMPOSITION OF GURU ARJAN,
GURU GRANTH, 684

Thus the people of an entire nation, albeit one that has no boundaries and yet spans continents, tune into a verse, a mystical and spiritual composition every day, and regardless of where they are, what they do, rich or poor, learned or lay, young or old, man, woman or child, of every nationality, every profession and vocation, all bow their heads and as never before in the Faith's five-century history, listen to their Guru in unison.

It is why Sikhs call themselves the *panth*, a nation united in prayer and service to humanity.

UNDERSTANDING NANAK

I have found from experience that we as human beings have a tough time in following simple instructions. The simpler they are, the more difficult it gets. We can decipher the most complex of codes and find our way through the most convoluted arguments, but given a straight-forward message we turn into navel-gazing philosophers and dig fiercely for hidden meanings or exceptions to the rule even when none exist.

The greatest of wisdom comes to us in little bites: Love thy neighbour. Thou shalt not kill. Thou shalt not steal ... You think we pay heed to these gems? You know the answer.

I'm no better.

I have had the good fortune of being born into Sikhi and have, for as long as I can remember, been enthralled by Nanak. It began with the *saakhis* (biographical stories) related to us as children at bedtime, but as I grew older and searched deeper, I realized that his life was the template, his poetry the GPS to all our goals.

With that knowledge in my pocket, I have wandered far and wide, still looking for 'answers'. It took a visit from a long lost friend a couple of decades ago that finally shook me awake and open my eyes to Nanak, to begin to understand him.

My friend was a Thai Bhikkhu – literally, a 'beggar' or 'one who lives by alms'. I say 'was' and not 'is' because he died a few years later. It is a term used to denote a Buddhist monk who lives a monastic life. He and I, close friends since I was a child despite our considerable age difference, had finally reconnected after three decades. We had lost touch when my family and I immigrated to Canada in 1971 when I was 21. I had finally tracked him down after a lengthy search which had taken me to Thailand. He was now living in a monastery in Los Angeles and was coming over for our first reunion.

One fine day he arrived in Guelph, a university town where I was living then, an hour's drive from Toronto, to spend a couple of weeks with us. Soon after we had picked him up at the airport and brought him home, I sat down with him to work out some logistical details. He was in his late 70s and I wanted to make sure we properly tended to his needs. One of my queries was: "What do you eat? And when?"

One meal a day, he said. Around noon, if possible. That's it. Nothing else in the morning or evening.

Okay, I said. Then tell me what you like, what you don't, what you can eat, what you can't, etc. I eat everything, he said. I have no preferences, no restrictions.

Sure, I said. But then, since you don't eat meat, what kind of vegetables and lentils would you like. He took my hand and smiled. "I do not eat anything special and I eat everything. I'll eat whatever you are eating. Please do not cook anything specifically for me. What you'll eat, I'll eat."

I shook my head. "That's impossible. We are Sikhs. We are meat-eaters. You are Buddhist and a monk. You are vegetarian. You can't eat what I normally eat. But that's no problem at all. We'll gladly restrict ourselves completely to vegetarianism while you're here. It entails no sacrifice. It'll do us good ..."

"But no," he said. "I observe no restrictions. If you'll eat meat, I will too. Gladly."

I was puzzled. Have I misunderstood Buddhism all along? I remembered from my youth that every time he visited us in Patna, my mother made it a point to serve him vegetarian food. I began to cross-examine him.

"Do you normally eat meat?" I asked him.

He shook his head.

"When was the last time you ate meat?" I asked him.

He smiled. And shrugged his shoulders.

"That's settled, then. No meat. We'll make a variety of lentils and vegetables if you won't tell us what you prefer."

"No, no, no!" he said, his nasal voice rising in distress. "You need to understand: as a bhikkhu, I go with the flow. We have no likes or dislikes. I do not crave for anything, nor do I reject anything. I will eat everything. The point is that you must not make a fuss, nor should you go out of your way to change things just for me."

He went on to explain that a bhikkhu lives on alms and alms alone. "Beggars are not choosers," he said. "That is my religion."

I stared at him in disbelief. He was being sincere, not just polite. I nodded but just couldn't get my head around what he had just told me. He would eat meat, he had said, to make sure he did not inconvenience us. Eating or not eating meat was not the issue. Being in harmony with those around him was the only thing that mattered to him.

Of course, we didn't pay heed to his request. Our diet became vegetarian for the duration of his stay. But he had planted a seed in my head which rattled me for a long, long time. Late that night, after I had left him in his bedroom for the night, I went to the room where we have *parkaash* of Guru Granth Sahib – our little home gurdwara – and I sought out the *shabad* in which Guru Nanak chides those who argue over whether it is better to eat meat or to be a vegetarian.

Suddenly it made perfect sense. There may be merit to both sides, Nanak tells us, but then asks, what is more important? What we eat or how we relate to each other?

My bhikkhu friend and I spent a lot of time together on this visit. We would get together again, once in Thailand as well where we traveled to remote monasteries together. But here in Guelph it was a time to span the three decades we had lost, to play catch up.

One day we walked to the river and sat on a bench looking at the ducks and geese in the water. I enjoyed being with him, not just our talks but also our quiet time together. What I liked about him on these occasions was that he did not have the need to be immersed in small-talk when we ran out of things to say. Quiet time was not a threat, not seen as a faux pas or a social failure. It was okay to say nothing even for long periods.

Looking at him engrossed in the antics of the birds, it hit me suddenly: what an odd couple we made sitting by the riverside. Not only were we two men who looked markedly different from everyone else in sight, we couldn't have been more different from each other: a Sikh and a Buddhist.

His head was shiny-bald, his chin clean-shaven. My head was covered with a turban, hiding a bun of unshorn hair. My chin was nowhere to be seen behind a thick beard.

I was dressed as worldly as you could get in this society. He, quite otherworldly in his saffron robe. He would never dress up in a business suit. I was expressly prohibited by my faith from donning a monk's garb.

I was a lawyer, a journalist and an activist. In the media almost everyday, for some reason or the other. He, a recluse with no active interest in the goings-on in the world; he had lived a life withdrawn from it all.

He a vegetarian, despite his protestations a few days earlier; I a carnivore and a meat-lover.

He a celibate; I in a long-term partnership and with a daughter in my household.

His faith required him to be a renunciate. My faith abhorred renunciation and demanded that I immerse myself in family life.

His faith required him to live off alms as an expression of total humility. My faith requires me to work as an act of total humility so that I can serve those who are in need with the fruits of my labour.

I, with all the entrapments of modern life. All of his worldly possessions were in a small shoulder bag back in our apartment.

Even our language was different. I spoke English fluently. He struggled with it, but it was the only language in which we could communicate with each other. I spoke without much of an accent; he was difficult to understand if you'd just met him.

There was nothing in his life-style that attracted me; there was no danger that I would ever abandon Sikhi to follow his path. There was nothing in my life-style that interested him, and there was no danger that he would ever emulate me.

Yet we were friends, life-long friends. Close, dear friends. I know I had missed him during the intervening three decades and more. In his words, he had too and had searched far and wide for me. When we finally met again it was like long-lost brothers. We had been separated not merely by a full generation but also by whole worlds and continents.

And it is that what brings me to Nanak. He suddenly makes perfect sense.

All he says – there is little else in the thousand pages of his compositions in the Guru Granth – is that though different from each other in a myriad of ways, we all emanate from the same source. And we reach our potential only when we enjoy each other. My bhikkhu friend and I could have found a hundred and one reasons to dislike each other or to stay away from each other. But since we tripped on none of them we never had a single disagreement.

My bhikkhu friend is no more. He died when a car he was in as a passenger was hit by an inebriated red-light jumper in LA. But he lives on in my heart because it was he who helped me begin my journey to find Nanak. To learn to understand Nanak.

To be a sikh, a seeker.

LIFE BEFORE THE PATKA

By the time I was five years old, my hair had grown down past my waist. The fact that my hair was unshorn and long, unlike that of any of the other boys (and some girls) who were with me in school at Mount Carmel Convent in Patna did not seem to bother me or anyone else.

It wasn't just that I looked different from the others who had their hair cut short. Mine was all the more remarkable in the way I wore it. It was neatly styled as a *gut* (essentially a back-braid; pronounced to rhyme with 'put', but with a soft 't'), somewhat like a french braid worn by some girls and women today.

It was a time, the early 1950s, before the *patka* was even heard of, probably even before it was invented. In fact it did not appear on the scene for another decade or two, and did not really catch on as a Sikh boy's headgear until the 1970s. It came to be widely used only years later.

There were two options for young Sikh boys then – the *joorrah* and the *gut*.

The joorrah consisted of the hair rolled and tied atop the head in a bun, like a top-knot. To keep it neat and in place, it was covered with a kerchief which was kept in place with a rubber-band.

The back-braid was more popular with middle-class families because it was neater and stayed relatively well-groomed through the rough and tumble of child play. And it stayed in place longer; a child could get by for much of the day having had his braid done in the morning.

The fact that I looked visibly different from my class-mates did not seem to be an issue. With them. Or with me. I knew that I was a Sikh, a Sardar, and that was how it was. Nobody questioned it. Nor did I. It was a fact of life. The nuns at Mount Carmel helped out if the braid ever threat-ened to unravel, but that was rare.

When I turned seven and graduated from Grade Three, I had to switch from the co-ed school I was in to an all-boys school. Much research and soul-searching had been done during the previous year to determine where I would move to for further schooling. My father and I travelled to many a city in North India checking out the popular schools: my parents were intent on finding the very best.

A number of options were on the table but when it came time to choose, distance became a hurdle. My parents discovered that neither of them was ready to send me, their eldest child and then their only son, too far away. They had lost two infant sons to illness, in quick succession, not long ago. As far as I was concerned I had no idea what I was getting into. Traveling to a distant place sounded exciting in itself.

We zeroed in on St. Michael's High School, located in the village of Kurji, more than a dozen miles north of the city of Patna where we lived. It was already by then a century-old establishment with a massive campus sprawling along the Ganges. Originally meant for the children of British officers serving the Raj, it was still run by Irish Christian Brothers and sported elaborate boarding facilities exclusively for boys.

So, come morning of Sunday, January 27, 1957, we drive through the gates of St. Michael's which would thereafter be my home off and on for the next eight years.

Amidst all the commotion – a dozen cars are disgorging families and luggage, while young boys already 'abandoned' by theirs look on wistfully – we head for the Principal's office where Brother Burke awaits us.

As pre-arranged, he has asked Sister Rita, the matron in-charge of the Junior Dormitory, to join us for a meeting. And George, the bespectacled, balding giant who I'll soon

111

get to know well as the chief hostel caretaker. The meeting has been called to help solve a dilemma.

Who will attend to the hair-washing and grooming of a seven-year old living in boarding school far from family? A number of options are discussed and after much hand-wringing a solution is found.

While parents are generally discouraged from visiting their children too frequently, my parents are given special dispensation: they will come once every week, probably on Sunday evenings, and no matter what I am involved in – study, sports, free play-time, etc. – I'll be excused to spend a couple of hours with them. My mother will then wash my hair, dry it and do the braid.

During the week I am to try and keep it neat, clean and dry, a feat I have to learn to accomplish through the two daily showers, the P.T. (physical training) in the morning, and the sports activities in the evening. If urgent help is needed, Sister Rita will assist.

And so it was.

I was the envy of my peers. At some unexpected hour on Sunday afternoon or evening, no matter where I was on the far-flung school grounds, I would hear some kid yell: "Tapi-i-i! Your people are here!"

Once a week I would get shampooed, scrubbed, towelled, speed-dried, disentangled, combed, oiled and greased, groomed, preened and pruned. Until I would finally stand there at dusk, shining and glistening, my hair tightly braided in a neat little bundle behind my head but reeking of coconut oil, with my weekly 'red-cross' supply of goodies in my hands, waving good-bye to my parents and siblings.

As I re-joined my friends either in the study hall, the refractory (dining hall), or dormitory, they would follow me with jealous eyes. When the lights went out later that night I would transform into the most popular boy around: my buddies would hurry through the shadows and crowd around my bed and we would hurriedly open the week's supply of my favourite *mitthhaee* (Punjabi home-made sweets), lovingly made at home and wrapped by my mother. We would go at the contents with a vengeance and wouldn't stop until all the containers were empty and licked clean, crumbs and all.

There was joy written all over our faces, reminiscent of Stalag XVII on Christmas Day, but with a smidgen of guilt, peppered with a tinge of melancholy. It would slowly dawn on us that it would be seven more long days before the next Sunday came along and my 'people' would visit again.

I would put the boxes away in the dark, silently promising myself for the umpteenth time to ration and stretch the goodies over the entire week the next time around.

Those promises, like New Year's resolutions later in life, were inevitably forgotten by the following Sunday.

113

CHANGE OF GUARD

It is well over five decades ago that I last changed the *karra* bracelet I wore on my right wrist until recently. I had come across one I really liked in Amritsar. It was simple, with no grooves or ornamentation. Steel. About a quarter of an inch deep across the diameter of its thickness, which was triangular, not round. Solid but not clunky. I weighed it on the palm of my hand. It was substantive yet not too heavy. I ran my fingers around its thickness, then along its entire circumference. It felt good.

I bought it, and asked the store-keeper if he could help me cut off the old one which sat on my right wrist. I had had it for a few years, having grown into it to the point that I could no longer slip it off. He had a wire cutter handy. It didn't take long. He handed it to me; I put it in my pocket, and slid the new one in its place. I liked it. So much so that it has been part of me ever since.

Years have flown by. From time to time I've seen new ones appear in the market or on people's wrists. Fancy, patterned ones. Some with inscriptions of *baani* on them. Or slogans. Then there are huge, thick, macho ones of *sarb loh* – 'all iron'.

Who could have thought there could be so many variations of a simple steel bracelet which is required to be, by definition, simple and un-ornate. Not showy or embellished. Not florid or ostentatious. Just a basic bracelet made of steel. Interesting designs, all those that I have come across through the years but none that I found appealing. You even find the occasional soul who brandishes one in gold, quite missing by a mile the very point of wearing it.

I have liked mine and never felt I would want to change it because I could never find one I liked as much. Or felt any need to change it for a new one. Being steel it has weathered well. It still has its dull shine. And looks as fashionable as ever, not that 'fashion' has anything to do with it. Though, to my utter surprise, I must say it has attracted endless compliments through the years. My favourite one is when I started dating a woman a few years ago and her two teenage children noticed the karra on my wrist one day and asked me about it.

I explained its significance and purpose.

"And you wear it all the time?" they asked.

I nodded.

"And all Sikhs do?" they asked.

I nodded.

"Cool," they chimed in unison, "what a fashionable religion!"

Before long, the three of them – mother, daughter and son – were each wearing one though they belonged to a different faith.

The one I have worn ever since I was 12 has never come off. Initially, I didn't need to take it off. Lately, I couldn't. Sure, I've grown in size and weight in the last half-a-century, but oddly my karra has merely become more snug and never too tight. It slides a couple of inches back and forth if I flail my arm but nothing in the world can induce it to slip off my wrist anymore. But it's never posed a problem.

I go through airport security check-points a dozen times every year. I tell the attendant about my karra before I step into the scanning machine. Invariably, they do a further scan with a hand-held monitor and off I go in a minute or two. Never been a problem.

And then there are the hospital nurses. Once every couple of years I find myself in a hospital to do a routine test which requires an anaesthetic, sometimes local, sometimes general. Invariably, each time during the prep, the nurse announces: "That's got to come off!"

"Do you need to?" I ask politely.

"Well, that's required. All metal has to be off," she tells me.

"Sure," I answer, "if you absolutely have to, I will. But do you absolutely need to?"

She shrugs her shoulders.

"Do we need to?" I repeat.

"Well," she finally gives in. "Let me see if I can put a tape around it."

Each time it means a minute's extra work for the nurse and then no one mentions it again.

I went through a similar procedure a couple of weeks ago. No one said a thing. When I woke up in the recovery room I noticed my karra was taped over. Now, just as the airport security personnel, most hospital staff know about Sikhs. That we wear a karra on our wrists. If and when asked, I've always told then: sure, cut it off if you absolutely need to. But, so far, there's never been a need to.

Until now.

I've noticed lately that if I over-indulge on occasion, such as at a wedding celebration the other day and gain a couple of pounds, my karra gets a bit more snug. So when I was at the Sacha Sauda Sikh store last week in Brampton, I looked around at the choice of karras. It took me a while but ultimately I found one I liked. Again, a simple and straight-forward one, with no bells and whistles. I asked the store-keeper for a magnet and tested it to make sure this one was indeed steel. I know that other metals could prove allergenic.

I brought it home. I decided it was time to graduate to a new one.

I felt nostalgic. I liked the old one: it was so much a part of me, having been with me every moment of my life literally for half a century and more. But I'm good with these things. If it has to go, it has to go.

Next question: how do I get it off? I thought long and hard about it. Finally, knew what to do. Went to Rod, the auto mechanic down the road who cares for my car. I explained to him my dilemma. He scratched his head for a while, intrigued by the challenge. "Never had this one before," he muttered.

A manual cutter wouldn't work: there was no room for the jaw to get under the metal. Rod tore through his garage looking for a solution, picking up one tool here, another implement there, but dismissing them one by one. Finally he came out with a hand-held gadget connected to a long rubber tube which disappeared into the room behind him.

"What is it?" I asked, getting a little edgy by this time, having had a few minutes to think about all that could go wrong.

"It's a high-speed cut-off tool," he said, waving a heavy-set wand which boasted a 3" circular saw-blade at one end. "It's pneumatically powered. At 18,000 rpm, it should do the trick."

I pulled my wrist back. I had a vision of my daughter who, at the age of 5, once had an accident and had cut off everything around her wrist: arteries, veins, tendons, nerves … It had been life-threatening and had required a team of a dozen surgeons from a variety of specializations to do all the repairs she needed.

We stared at the tool for a few long moments, and then at my wrist, and then back at the blade.

"18,000 rpm, you say?" I whispered.

Rod found an inch wide, half-an-inch thick strip of steel to slide under the karra to protect my flesh and bone.

"There'll be sparks. And it'll get hot. You don't want to burn yourself. Or your shirt."

He brought out a glove. I slipped it on, and slid back my shirt sleeve and covered my arm with a rag. My eyes were glued on the saw-blade hovering over my wrist. I did a quick mental calculation as to how long it would take to get to the hospital if I needed to.

18,000 rpm it was. There were fireworks accompanied by an ear-piercing, whining clamour. I closed my eyes. Steel doesn't give easily. It took a full minute. We took a break. I dipped my hand in a bucket of water to cool off the metal. Then we went at it again. Finally, it had been cut in half. The karra, I mean.

I'm now the proud owner of two karras, one a life-long companion now bisected, and the other which I expect will keep me company for the rest of my days. And Rod has a story to tell his Baptist friends in church next Sunday where he preaches as an assistant pastor.

I am left ruminating on why this karra, the old and the new, has been so important to me. Sure, it is one of the Five K's that I wear as articles of faith. I know of all its meanings and nuances and its symbolism. Yup, it is meant to symbolize God the Infinite by its perfect geometric shape, a circle which has no beginning, no end. Steel is strong, its relative timelessness easily withstands the elements. It is worn on the right wrist – or left, if it is the hand you use most readily – to remind you to be moderate, restrained and balanced in all that you do in your daily life. And so on ...

But there's got to be more, I say to myself. Surely there's a reason why it means so much to me, a person who abhors jewellery. I love watches and collect finely-designed models but hate wearing one. Even when I was married for a stint of eight years or so once, I couldn't stand wearing the wedding ring or those that my parents gifted me on the occasion.

But I like the karra and its permanence.

I've given it much thought these last few days and have come to realize that it has been a source of immense strength for me. Not in some airy-fairy, hocus-pocus manner, not because it is metal, and not because it is round, or on my wrist. But because of my personal and very private relationship with it. It proves to me that I am capable of commitment through thick and thin, that I can cut through trends and fashions, whims and fads, and remain steadfast with an idea, with a belief, with a conviction. After all, I've been wearing one non-stop from shortly after I was born, to this day 69 years later and will, I expect, wear it when I'm finally in my coffin.

It gives me confidence – direct, personal and private – that I can do anything I want without having to be blindly adherent to an ideology. That once the concept becomes part of me, then the idea is all, the rest is nothing.

I have realized that there is nothing worldly that I have or have had which comes close to the karra. It is of no worldly value: this new one I bought for less than a dollar. In a way, it does nothing, it says nothing, it represents nothing.

Yet, it is me in more ways than I have ever imagined.

IDENTITY

One of the most significant things that European immigration brought to North America was confusion. It began with Columbus. Driven by greed – not an interest in the scenery, anthropology or spirituality – he feverishly searched for India. But, he was also not the brightest of lights. With a twist of irony that only history is capable of, he landed in the Americas. Believing he had arrived in India, he promptly named the natives 'Indians'.

Ever since confusion has reigned and continues to this very day. We Sikhs have inherited this legacy and are left to grapple with the ensuing stupidities.

Contemporaneous to Columbus' drooling for the riches of India, the Sikh Faith was born in Punjab, an area lying in the northern region of the sub-continent. In the centuries that followed, Europeans went about busily lusting for and 'discovering' various lands. Yes, 'discover' even though full-fledged civilizations had been inhabiting these places from time immemorial.

They thought they'd arrived in India and named all that they saw as 'India' or the 'Indies'. Then proceeded to re-name everyone they came across this land they claimed they had 'discovered'. Henceforth they would all be 'Indians'.

That created a problem. How do you distinguish the Indians of the Americas from the Indians of the subcontinent, for example? Hence, Red Indians, East Indians, West Indians ...

In 1897, my ancestors – Sikhs from Punjab – reciprocated by 'discovering' the Americas. Now, we need to remember that by this time the British Empire had had a substantial presence – not unlike 'Jabba the Hutt' of Star Wars fame, I might add – on the subcontinent for almost 300 years. They knew the Sikhs well, especially since they had been major players in the Raj during much of the 19th century.

Oddly though, despite the close relationship, the British and other Europeans had a lot of difficulty remembering how to spell 'S-I-K-H'. I jest not ... after all, it was before they discovered ginseng and ginkgo biloba!

A simple four letter-word, believe it or not, 'Sikh' has been mis-spelled by our friends in no less than 21 – yes, TWENTY-ONE – different ways. You don't have to take my word; Dr. Ganda Singh, the great Sikh scholar, has culled them from his research and lists them as follows:

Seck

Seeck

Seek

Seick

Seik

Seikh

Seyque

Shik

Shikh

Sic

Sic'hs

Sick

Sicke

Sicque

Siek

Siekh

Sik

Sike

Sique

Syc

Syck

If this doesn't prove that the Europeans are indeed a superior civilization and were gifted to us from outer space, nothing else will. Who else could do so much with just four letters, even daring to add or switch one or two willy nilly, and come up with such brilliant variations?

As Sikh immigration trickled in, people here in Canada – an intrinsic part of the British Empire that freely shared its booty – struggled with how to refer to the immigrants. Of course, calling them by their actual name simply would not do. That would be too mischievous.

Mackenzie King, an influential bureaucrat and budding politician during this period, and a committed racist, promptly insulted them by labelling them 'Hindoos'.

You need to know one other thing about our Mackenzie King. Riding on the racism tiger, he later became Prime Minister of Canada. He was the author of the term 'White Man's Country' but he wasn't talking about snow, trust me. Not long after he died, his diaries were discovered and they revealed that he conducted all his affairs, including of the Canadian Government and Parliament, under the close guidance of his dead mother who communicated to him through the ether via his dog, who was alive and reportedly 'conversed' with him everyday. I swear none of this is made up. This is pure, unadulterated history. This is the stuff with which these lands were 'civilized', to borrow a term from George W. Bush.

Then in the decades that followed Mackenzie King Canada discovered, first, that women were actually 'persons' and should be given the right to vote. Second: that Sikhs, Chinese, Japanese and others, too, were 'persons' and should be given equal rights. At that point, my people

– Sikh-Canadians – were once again thrown within the general rubric of, first, 'Asians', and then, back to 'East Indians'.

The post-World-War II period saw the world become smaller. We learned more about each other as some of the veils of ignorance were torn down. Thus by the end of the dastardly twentieth century we had entered a new age of enlightenment. Bureaucrats finally acknowledged that it would indeed help us all if we knew more about the true demographics of this country. Statistics Canada decided to ask a few more questions in the census. It released its report ... and dropped a bombshell.

My daughter and I – and all Sikh-Canadians, almost half-a-million of them – are now referred to as 'South Asians.

The English are English, not West Europeans. The French are French, not Mid-West-Coastal Europeans. But Sikhs and other Indians, as well as Pakistanis, Sri Lankans, Bangladeshis, Nepalese, Bhutanese, Sikkimis, and Lord knows who else, are henceforth South Asians!

South Asians?

I own a colossal dictionary. It has 460,000 entries, 2764 pages. It is so heavy it has to sit on a solid oak pedestal. And, you know, there is no entry for 'South Asian'.

Imagine. After a modern and fully-recorded history of five-and-a-half centuries on this planet, and 121 years in Canada, my people have now been given a designation that has no meaning, no history, no pride, no commonality, no language, no flag, no literature, no tradition, no heritage. Nothing.

Just think about it: when you hear the term 'South Asian', does it bring tears of pride to your eyes? Does it warm the cockles of your heart when you hear the words uttered? Just like an Englishman's when he conjures up Henry V's oration or when he hears the word 'England'. Or the way our heart swells when we Sikhs think of Ranjit Singh or sing our national anthem, 'Deh shiva bar mohe ihai ...'

Will somebody in some bureaucracy explain to me, please, who are the 'South Asians' and why are they being bunched together? Or under any alien rubric. Why are we labelled Asians in some countries, Blacks in others, Coloreds in some. And South Asians ... ?

What do the Chinese and the Japanese have in common with my people, in a census? In the same context, what do blacks from around the world have in common with my people? And, for that matter, what do the Sri Lankans and the Bangladeshi, or the Sikh and the Tamil, have in common that demands they be thrown into a common, faceless category, while statistics pertaining to the Irish, Scots, Germans, Italians, etc., are collected without any difficulty and regardless of the expense? If we are South Asians, why aren't they just Europeans and the Jews Middle-Easterners?

Is there mischief involved in this, or is it merely negligence and/or ignorance? Or simple, unadulterated stupidity?

Here's some more food for thought. In and across the diaspora, Sikhs are a majority in the context of people from the subcontinent. Furthermore, once outside the artificial construct of India left behind by the fleeing Brits in 1947, the component communities fragment as soon as their members get off the boat ... into Bengalis, Gujratis, Tamils, Marathis, Malyalees, Kashmiris, Keralites.

On the other hand, Sikhs, despite all the challenges in the world, have remained relatively united or as united as it is humanly possible under the circumstances. Therefore, living in this truly democratic countries where resources are doled out in accordance to numbers and votes, it doesn't help if you're bunched together with the *desis* (the amorphous glob called 'Indians'). And it doesn't help if you belong to this caste or that, or that you have an uncle from your village in some 'high' place. All that count are numbers and votes.

Hence, maybe, the invention of this hitherto unknown creature called 'South Asian'. The desis ride on the coat-tails of all the communities – especially the Sikhs – and garner the resources then proportioned to the whole lot. Sadly, the resources then get applied to the vested interests of a few greedy ones.

For example, go to any Department of Indian Studies in any university and see if there is even a trace of anything Sikh in its environs. Go to any function held with the involvement of India's diplomats, the fellas who are meant to represent *all* Indians, and all you'll see will be Hindu icons and Hindu worship of strange idols called devis and devtas, as if the Constitution of India was secretly changed one night under cover of darkness and the country has now officially become a land of idol-worshippers. No respect or consideration for, no sensitivity to Sikhs, Muslims, Christians and Jews whatsoever.

Thus, they've learnt to stand on our shoulders but remain pigmies at our expense, whilst we are nowhere to be seen or heard in their corridors.

It is time we stood tall and proud as Sikhs ... undiluted, unadulterated Sikhs! If we are to be counted like the others, we are SIKHS, not Indians, not Punjabis, not East Indians, not Asians, not Blacks, not Coloreds ... just Sikhs.

This is not being parochial or provincial. Either we go all the way with Guru Nanak's message, all of us – that the 'Whole Human Race is One' – and label ourselves as nothing but Humans. Or, if we indeed need a breakdown for administrative purposes, let's be thorough and accurate.

So, if you really want to know:

I am a Canadian, like other Canadians are. Those like me who follow the high ideals of Sikhi are Sikhs, exactly the way you are Christian or Jewish or whatever. We are of Punjabi origin and proud of it the way you are of Welsh or Italian origin, or whatever. We speak English the way you do, sometimes better. But my mother tongue is Punjabi, just as yours is English, or French, or whatever.

If you are Italian-American, Afro-American, English-Canadian, French-Canadian, etc., remember ... we are Sikh-American, Sikh-Canadian, Sikh-Briton, Sikh-Kiwi, Sikh-Indian, Sikh-Aussie, etc.

For heaven's sake, categories such as Chinese, Korean, English, Japanese, etc., I can comprehend. How on earth did you get to 'South Asian'? And why? If a country's census machinery can count the English, Scots and Welsh separately without lumping them together as 'British', why should the dozen even more clearly demarcated communities which have far greater numbers be counted as a shapeless glob called 'South-Asian' merely because they hail from the same subcontinent?

No wonder they still confuse us Sikhs. This time around with 'Muslims'. Sometimes, Lord forbid, even with 'Hindus'.

Pray, who's to blame?

WHEN DOES CHARDI KALAA CLICK IN?

Every now and then I'm asked the question: don't you find it depressing dealing with the daily mess in the world? A number of people posed it in tandem the other day after a news report evidencing that the community's detractors back in India are continuing their shenanigans against Sikhs full speed by belting out their usual propaganda.

"Doesn't that make you depressed?" they lamented. Not really.

I wake up early in the morning and step outside to inhale the fresh air, and I see insects on the ground and in the air – vermin of every kind, actually – scurrying for cover as the sun rises. Does it make me depressed, seeing them around, doing their handiwork? Not really.

They do their thing. As long as we get to do our thing,

all's well with the world. Is there anything new about the mischief emanating from corrupt and sinking regimes? They've always been miserable and they continue to be miserable. When the Indians mess up things too much, they whine and whimper and implore Sikhs to jump into the fray and clean up the place a bit, which they will do because it is in their DNA to serve humanity. Sikhs then go back to their lives. But again, once the lights are out, the roaches will be out again … and so the cycle of life continues.

I do not find the presence of evil around me depressing for the simple reason that it is a fact of life. It's always been around and as long as we do nothing meaningful it'll be around.

When our Gurus walked the earth, there was no dearth of evil men. Guru Nanak witnessed the Mughal invader Babur rape, pillage and plunder. Guru Arjan was tortured by one of the tyrant's successors. Guru Tegh Bahadar was beheaded, also by one of Babur's descendants. So, if evil flourished while our Guru were around, why should we expect scoundrels not to be present when our Gurus have been gone for centuries. They crucified Jesus when he walked the earth. So, why should they be any better when he's been gone for two millennia?

I've learnt to accept it all as a fact of life, as something we have to deal with on a daily basis, but not something I'm willing to get depressed over.

Here's how I handle evil. I figure out what I can do best to thwart it, do my bit, do my best, and then let the chips fall where they may. Once I've done my fair share, I have no difficulty sleeping at night.

However, I can see why some who will do nothing – nothing with their skills or talents or wealth or time – except maybe express opinions on what others should do to ward off the evil-doers, I can understand why they get depressed and why they lose sleep at night.

They'll even cheer you on to be in *chardi kalaa* ... but will still not lift a finger to do anything meaningful. Chardi Kalaa, the Sikh concept of eternal optimism, is not a slogan. It's not a song. It's not a movie title. It's an approach to life. It's not something you feel when you've won the lottery. It's how you think and behave when you have no money in the bank. It's not the glow you bask in when they give you an honour. It's how you deal with it when they choose to dishonour you, for good reason or bad.

Chardi kalaa is not for good times. It is for times when the going's tough and things don't seem to be going your way.

There is a constant din I hear from many a good soul lamenting where Sikhs are heading. And then I look at them, searching for the Sikhi in themselves and can't seem to find a trace of it. You can't poke yourself in the eyes and then complain that the world has turned dark.

135

No, there is nothing wrong with Sikhi. What's wrong is what some of us are doing or not doing. Let's not blame the community or Sikhi or the times. I for one think Sikhi is as glorious as ever. True, Sikhdom needs some servicing, but despite its challenges I feel it is doing better than ever before. Young Sikhs by the thousands dazzle me today with their commitment to Sikhi at a level I have seen only in rare individuals in the past. More Sikhs are now actively thinking about their Sikhi and how to live it right than ever before in history.

Sure there are many of us who have fallen off the wagon and many more who fall far short of the ideals. But there are so many more who are riding high. When was the last time you met a Christian or a Jew or a Hindu or a Muslim who lives his or her life truly according to his faith?

Let me tell you of how I have fared in my search. I have met but a handful of Christians in recent years who live the life of a true Christian. The same goes with Jews. The last time I met a Hindu who practices his faith the way he/she is supposed to by its stated values, was a while ago. Muslims? I've met a couple, but no more.

Sikhs? I could instantly cite you dozens that I admire and yearn to emulate. Trust me, it's not because I know more Sikhs because I don't: most of the people I have dealings with are non-Sikhs. I live in a society where Christians, Jews and Muslims outnumber Sikhs … and Hindus number about the same. And, in my line of work, I get to interact with far more people of every faith than any average person does.

The bottom line: Sikhs and Sikhdom aren't doing too badly, despite the grievous challenges we face today.

It's no reason to be complacent, though. But also, there's no reason to get depressed. We mustn't lose sight of the fact that we live in a brave new world where everything is up for grabs. The rules, traditions and conventions that we grew up with have all been thrown out of the window. Modern technology has taken the awe out of everything that hitherto wowed us, and has given us permission to question and tear down anything and everything without having to have any qualifications to do so.

It's a new ball-game and we Sikhs, like all other communities, are reeling from the new lack of rules.

So be it.

It's time for Chardi Kalaa!

MOVING FORWARD – OR SLIDING BACKWARD?

I was not surprised to see Rajesh Mehta at the gurdwara. I knew he occasionally attended the Sunday morning services and sometimes even dropped in at other hours. After the service we headed for the langar hall together. We are close friends and there was a lot to talk about and catch-up this time around. During a lull in the conversation – it must have been when I was engrossed in lapping up the heavenly daal – the discussion took an unusual turn.

"You know, Sher, I'm a Hindu but I love coming here because the kirtan and being amidst the sangat brings me peace. But I've often wondered: do you ever go to a mandir? Any Hindu temple?"

139

"Why do you ask, Rajesh?" I was doing my lawyer thing, I guess, answering a question with a question to bide time.

"It just hit me ... I've never seen you at my mandir. And I've never heard you talk about visiting one, ever. So just curious ..."

"Well," I said, "I have visited the most famous of them all at Badrinath in the upper Himalayas. I was in the vicinity, a mere two days' trek away, when I was in Hemkunt and took a diversion to the temple. Have you been there?"

"No, I haven't. You are lucky you had the opportunity."

I continued, thinking I was on a roll: "And I've been to Hardwar and Benares and Gaya ... all major centres of Hindu pilgrimage. And umpteen ones in Bali and Nepal. You know I love visiting any place of worship."

"No, no," piped in Rajesh. "I didn't mean as a tourist. Like me ... the way I pop in here every time the spirit moves me. I wonder if you ever go to a Hindu mandir the way I come to a gurdwara."

I went quiet, contemplative quiet, not sure what I should say.

"For example, when was the last time you were in a mandir?"

I thought about it and shrugged my shoulders.

Rajesh: "H-m-mm. So tell me, have you ever been to a mandir in all the years you've been living in Canada? Thirty years, forty years ...?"

I could see where he was heading and didn't want to go there. I knew he knew the answer but I wasn't willing to be drawn into a discussion on the issue. He looked at me and elbowed me gently. "Never? You haven't gone to a mandir here once, have you?"

I shook my head in agreement.

"How come?" I knew this was coming.

"I don't know, Rajesh. I really don't know. No particular reason, I guess."

Mercifully he dropped the subject. We got up and headed for the door. I was relieved because Rajesh is dear to me and I didn't want to say anything that would turn into an argument over religion. Or hurt his sentiments. Ever since, and its been several months since that exchange, my thoughts have gone back to his question. I have searched deep into myself for the answer. I too have wanted to know the answer because it was true that I do not enjoy going to a mandir, except as a tourist. Looks like I've subconsciously avoided going to one. It has no spiritual draw for me.

I've struggled long and hard for an honest answer to why it is so. And when I found one, it didn't surprise me even though it took me a while to be comfortable with it and accept it as the very part of my being: what shapes me, guides me, directs me in all that I do. I haven't dared to share this discovery of myself with Rajesh because I fear that he may not welcome it or it may hurt him a bit. I value our friendship too much for me to risk treading on what is dear to him. But if I ever have the courage to give him the answer one day here's what it'll be:

Well Rajesh, here's what I think. I think it is easy for you to come to a gurdwara even though you are a Hindu. Each time you step over the portal of a gurdwara you step five centuries into the future and into a world which has peeled off thousands of years of onion layers of ritual and superstition to get to a simple and direct relationship between oneself and one's spiritual needs.

On the other hand every time I find myself stepping into a mandir I see myself stepping back half a millennium into the past, leaving behind generations of human and spiritual progress, of all of the shedding of historical baggage that our ancestors have helped to do away with. Standing in front of the idols and surrounded by the rituals and superstitions, I would feel a stunning sense of betrayal to all that I have inherited and learned since my birth.

I pass no judgement in what you do in a mandir or as part of your faith and beliefs. But I certainly know for sure that it is not a path that I wish to tread. It's a choice of moving forward with five hundred years of progress or sliding back five hundred years of regression.

Rest assured that though I choose a different path than yours, this path requires me to protect YOUR right to practice YOUR faith as YOU deem fit within YOUR mandirs and anywhere else you choose, no matter who – I or anyone else – finds it difficult to understand or follow. To defend your right to the death as did our Ninth Master in Chandni Chowk in the heart of Delhi and as countless others have done since then and through the centuries.

It gives me no great pleasure to tell you that my knees simply will not bend, my head will just not bow before an idol, no matter how beautiful, how tall, how rich …

I believe that no other entity – man, woman, child or object – can help solve my problems or wash my sins away. There's no prophet or priest, sant or saint, idol or icon, who can bring me prosperity, stave off evil, punish my enemies, get me a promotion, bring me wealth, or guarantee me salvation, etc. Life doesn't work by proxy for me. There are no interceders for me, not even Guru Nanak or Guru Gobind Singh. All that I have going for me is the way they have shown and which I try to follow and if I do what I have to do, I will be able to achieve what they themselves achieved.

Yes, I pray for grace but from no flesh or stone or icon. I need no broker. God – call Him/Her what you will – for me is not hiding behind gimmicks, like the Great and Powerful, Supreme Wizard of the Kingdom of Oz. He is as accessible

– as directly and easily – as a father and mother, sister and brother, friend and lover. It's a very personal relationship. Therefore I need to walk the walk by myself. I will gladly pay for my wrongs and learn from them. I will benefit from the good that I do. The gurdwara that I go to – and not all gurdwaras fit that bill – facilitates my journey. A mandir has nothing to offer me on the journey I have chosen.

I am not and never have been blessed with the gift of certainty in all the things that I believe in and follow. I know that, more often than not, I'll be wrong and from time to time I'll have to regroup with all of my faculties and start all over again. Accordingly what I have stated above is simply how I feel and what I believe in honestly.

I shared it all with a Sikh friend the other day to see if it met the test of the light of the day. He pounced on me as soon as I finished and instantly accused me of betraying all that Sikhi stood for by being intolerant of other faiths. I begged to differ.

Sikhi demands that I be tolerant and more. Actually, not just tolerant but respectful of other faiths. Which I am. I revel in the devotion and faith and commitment others show in their respective ways to their spiritual path and get inspiration from it. But Sikhi at no point requires me to delve in those practices as a show of support or empathy.

The passionate verses of the Bhagats Namdev, Ravidas and other great Hindu souls included in the Guru Granth drench me in joyful tears and inspire me along my own path, but at no point do I then adopt the very rituals they delved in and overcame. Moreover, I do not criticize Hindu or any other forms of worship. I do not advocate any opposition to it amongst those who practice them. I neither proselytize nor preach.

Yes, I do try to discern for myself and share with my fellow-Sikhs what is true, unadulterated Sikhi and what isn't, and I try to add to the dialogue for those who wish to know about Sikhi.

And yes, I do tear off the veils of *pakhand* (hypocrisy) and fraud no matter which mantle the scoundrel throws on his shoulders – Sikh, Hindu, Muslim, Christian, Buddhist, Jew or whatever – but never, NEVER do I give myself or anyone the license to decry another's religion.

Thus, for example, it is no right of mine to question the worship of idols BY Hindus. But I do question when the worship of idols is used as a front for insurance scams by insuring those very idols for millions of dollars. I do not question the Hindu practice of worshipping a multiplicity of gods and goddesses, but I do take umbrage with charlatans who prey on those very human sentiments to scam millions of dollars from their devotees thus blinded by their devotion. And so on and so forth.

Someday I hope I'll have the courage to tell dear Rajesh to his face my answer to his question. In the meantime I await your judgements.

THE CROWNING

The human male from time immemorial has been subjected to a whole variety of rites of passage as he morphs
from child to adult, boyhood to manhood. Some societies such as the warrior communities have required him to
prove himself by surviving extreme feats of physical and
mental endurance. Others have subjected him to a period
of extreme privation and deprivation as in the life of a
novice monk.

The female of the species have also been subjected to
parallel practices, but mostly they have been designed by
males who had their own, selfish interests in mind.

Sikhism too has its rite of passage prescribed for all of
its adherents as each aspires to its ideal: that of the Saint-
Soldier. But its principal rite differs from others in that it is
open to both sexes and it requires no external feats. What
it requires is passage into maturity through an internal

awareness of one's role in society as a Sikh and a deep-seated, personal commitment to it.

The ceremony itself is called *Dastaar Sajaani* … The Crowning. That is, adorning oneself with a turban.

The dastaar is known by many names … *puggri, saafa* and, of course, the turban. The Sikh turban is different from all of those worn by other communities currently or in the past. It is distinguished by its carefully sculpted lines and neatness. It is not a mere head-covering or hat, or part of a dress, costume or uniform. It is not just a tradition or a mere article of faith. It is all of these and much, much more.

It harks back to the crown worn by kings and queens. There were two main implications to the wearing of a crown. First, the wearer, King or Queen, was upon being crowned answerable to no man or woman, only to God. Secondly, the crowned head signified the wearer's life-long and primary duty to protect and serve his/her subjects.

The Sikh turban imposes the very same two ramifications on its wearer: he or she is answerable in spiritual matters to no man or woman, only to the One God, the Lord of all creation; and that it is his or her duty to protect the weak, serve the poor, tend to the needy … all in preference to his/her own needs. That is, the Sikh is to always work for *sarbat da bhalla*, the good of all humanity.

It is this role that the young Sikh accepts as he dons the turban for the first time and thenceforth gradually takes on the duties and responsibilities of life within society. I should point out here that even though the Sikh turban is primarily worn by the male, more and more women are wearing it nowadays. Hence, the Dastaar Sajaani ceremony applies equally to the female who chooses to wear one. 'He' and 'she' are used here interchangeably.

This, coupled, with a life of prayer – not removed from it – is the way of the Sikh. And all of it is captured symbolically in the simple act of donning a turban.

There is more. Not unlike the American way but in fact much more so, each Sikh revels in standing out in a crowd. Not to inflate the ego but to stand tall and confident. You can spot a turban-wearing Sikh instantly even if he is one amidst a thousand others.

As I have said, the Sikh stand-out-edness is not meant to be an egocentric exercise. He is required by definition to be *niraala* and *nyaara* – unique, special, excelling, standing-out, out-standing. And yet steeped in humility throughout.

So that she remembers and is constantly reminded by others of her civic role. So that he or she can never shirk or hide from it even when it becomes unfashionable or dangerous to be identified as a Sikh. There is no room for cowardice for a Sikh.

He is a Sardar, she a Sardarni ... a leader! These are the honorifics traditionally used for every Sikh male or female instead of 'Mr' or 'Mrs'. He is a Singh, a lion; she a Kaur, a princess.

Every Sikh is *savaa lakh*. That is, equivalent to the proverbial 125,000. An army of one.

Every Sikh is to be gentle and sweet as a sparrow but ever ready to take on hawks and overcome them. And so on and on go the multiple gifts and blessings that come with the turban crown. It is the initiation into this phase of life symbolized by the first adorning of the head with a turban – to be worn throughout one's life thereafter – that we celebrate by joining the young man or woman and the family in the beautiful ceremony called Dastaar Sajaani.

The color of the turban has no special significance. No color is auspicious. No color is taboo. My daughter once quipped: "Just make sure it matches with your tie ... and underwear."

The turban consists of a long piece of cloth – fine, light cotton – approximately 5-6 meters (18 feet) long, about a meter (or yard) wide. There are, of course, some variations of this. Once learnt how to tie it, it takes no more than a minute or two to do. The fabric is required to always be unstitched to ensure that it is freshly wrapped everyday so that it is, unlike a hat, aired and clean throughout the time it is worn. Also, because it is made of cotton, it breathes, which helps avoid undue sweating on the scalp.

I recall when my nephew Harjaap Singh in Florida went through this regal rite of passage into manhood. The inaugural adornment was with the help of a parent as well as a respected Elder from the community.

The ceremony took place in the presence of the Sikh Scripture, the Guru Granth, which is treated like a living person in the tradition of The Living Word. Hence, all the accoutrements of royalty around it: the Palki (throne), the attendant, the Chaur Sahib (fly whisk), the Chandova (canopy) above. And the fact that we all sit on the carpet facing it, cross-legged or with our feet not pointing towards it, in respectful silence and deference. Earlier, we will have left our shoes outside and entered with our heads covered.

All of these being the decorum and protocol traditionally followed in a royal court. Why? Because we are in the court of our Guru, our Spiritual Guide and Teacher.

All Sikh ceremonies are basic, simple and straight-forward with virtually the same service, regardless of the occasion: readings and singing from the scripture. Little else. This is true for congregations that gather in joy or in sorrow, to celebrate or to commemorate or to merely start or end a normal day.

On Harjaap's big day, there were readings from the Guru Granth. Some singing of hymns. Some words spoken to explain to the young man his new role and responsibilities. Blessings from his parents and elders. A congregational prayer to bless him on his path ahead. Followed by a sacrament called Karraah Parshad, a simple pudding made of flour, butter and sugar. And langar, the communal meal in which all present, Sikh and non-Sikh, partook. A community is at its best when it breaks bread together.

It was indeed a very special day in the life of young Sardar Harjaap Singh.

A BEAUTIFUL THING

I was in my teens when I, along with my sister Davinder Kaur, took Amrit. I found the ceremony life-transforming with so many factors adding to its magic: the fact that we were in Gobind Ghat high up in the upper Himalayas, almost in the shade of Mount Hemkunt, was one particularly notable blessing.

Another was that the Punj Pyarey, the five who would administer Amrit to us in order to initiate us into the Khalsa, were respected stalwarts of the community: Sardar Sant Singh, then head of the Chief Khalsa Diwan (at a time when it was very much a venerable institution); Sardar Joginder Singh Mann, a highly regarded community leader; Bhai Mohan Singh Raagi from Bombay (my favourite *kirtaniya* then); Sardar Shamsher Singh who headed the Hemkunt Foundation; and my father, Sardar Ishar Singh.

Both Davinder and I were old and mature enough to be in sympathetic resonance with the spiritual ambience of both the ceremony and our surroundings, and were certainly ready to take on the full discipline of the faith including the wearing of the kirpan.

Taking on this article of faith was a special moment loaded with a sense of heavy responsibility. It is difficult to explain the feeling of donning a kirpan upon taking Amrit: it seemed to inject and infuse a glow of self-confidence and a sense of commitment, all in an instant. It is not the kind of experience that can be reduced to words or conveyed to another. It is experiential and of a spiritual and personal nature, something that has to be tasted first-hand. But a caveat: it can't be done by simply donning a kirpan. The pre-requisite of taking on the life-style and discipline is an essential and mandatory first step before the act of taking on the kirpan.

It has nothing to do with the kirpan being a weapon, because it is not one. It is neither a defensive weapon nor one for aggression. It is an article of faith, no more, no less, encapsuling the central principles of Sikhi.

Some ask me what I would do if I was attacked by a stranger. Would I then use it to defend myself? Wouldn't that make it a weapon? Well, if someone attacked me and I felt I was, or others around me were in danger, I would grab the first thing I could put my hands on to fend off the assailant: a pen in my pocket, a pencil on the table, a paper-weight, the Napoleon bust on my desk, a chair ... anything. Would that make any of them a weapon? Should they all be banned?

Right from the start this began to weigh on me, the fact that the kirpan is so important an icon of our beliefs and intrinsically tied to our duties and obligations, both spiritual and temporal. If it is to be worn on the person as a constant reminder of who we are and what we stand for, surely it should be easy and convenient to wear, and pleasant to touch and hold, even to look at.

What haunted me in particular was what I had been taught as part of my Sikh upbringing: that all things representing and standing for truth must, by definition, be beautiful and that all things beautiful are by definition imbued with truth.

Why then, I was troubled from the very outset, was my kirpan not a thing of beauty? The ones available in the marketplace were crudely made and certainly none gave me pleasure when held in my hand. By no stretch of the imagination were they a delight to look at. It was sadly, like most things made in India today, roughly the right shape, had the general design and configuration, but little more. I must confess I wore the kirpan uncomfortably but only because I was unhappy that I was carrying around something that was not aesthetically up to the role it had been assigned. If it was going to be part of my spiritual journey I expected it to inspire me and uplift me.

I searched far and wide for one that I liked. I was directed to the Kashmiri wood-carved hilt and sheath. It was okay,

155

certainly better than the one I already had, but still not befitting an icon. I continued searching.

The search for my holy grail has spanned decades and stretched across continents. In 2004, there was an encouraging whiff of fresh air when Victorinox, the makers of the renowned Swiss Army Knife, launched a kirpan which was a marked improvement on everything available then from the mothership in Punjab. For some unknown reason, it didn't catch on. Probably the steep price. Wish they had stuck to the project; sales would have increased gradually and the price would have plummeted.

Still no relief in sight.

And then Sardar Jot Singh Khalsa appears on my horizon. ('Jot' is pronounced as in 'coat' but with a soft 't'). I hold in my hand a kirpan crafted by him and his Khalsa Kirpans and I can say to you with the glee and excitement of an Indiana Jones that I have found my grail. To put it succinctly, it – is – a – thing – of – beauty.

It is not very big, just the size I need. A bit more than 6 inches long, both the kirpan and its accompanying leather sheath. Together, an inch thick. An inch and a half wide. It's simple in design but exquisite to look at, a joy to hold in the hand and to feel the gentle weight of the metal, the warm texture of the leather. It balances beautifully, indicating that a lot of thought has gone into its production and design.

I wear it on my waist belt. It sits on the side effortlessly and never interferes with my movements whether I'm sitting or standing. It is snug enough to feel part of me. The kirpan and the sheath have been blended together masterfully.

A reminder: I have merely opted for the simplest one and love it immensely even though I covet each of the others in Jot Singh's extensive catalogue of masterpieces. If you venture into the full-length sword-size kirpans, the kind that is part of Anand Kaaraj, the Sikh wedding ceremony, Jot Singh's treasure-chest runneth over.

I am of the firm belief that we should honour and embrace our icons and articles of faith in the most beautiful manifestations that our respective means allow: the palki, chaur, degh, baata, chandova and chhabba, rumalas, gutka, karra, kanga, even the body of our Guru Granth Sahib, to name but a few. They don't have to be expensive or ornate but if we can afford to make them as works of art we should create the finest examples we possibly can. Not to idolize them or turn them into objects of worship but to show our reverence for things that symbolize our values and precepts.

Jot Singh's creation has given me endless joy. I hope every Sikh household, not just each amritdhari Sardar and Sardarni, will have the opportunity to have this important icon of Sikhi in their homes just as diligently as each is expected to have Guru Granth Sahib grace them. And when doing so, I hope each will put in that extra effort to seek out a thing of beauty to fulfill that role.

Don't get me wrong. Even things created cheaply and inexpensively can be exquisitely beautiful. But it'll only happen if we demand of ourselves or from those who create them, that we turn them into objects of art.

After all, " 'Beauty is truth, truth beauty,' – that is all ye know on earth, and all ye need to know." [John Keats]

HOLA MOHALLA

Our Gurus began a formidable task five centuries ago of not only transforming society on the subcontinent but also introducing ideas which would prove revolutionary for all people across the globe. A few of their approaches were already subscribed to by communities here and there but mostly through mere lip-service.

Some of the concepts were new to human thought and would eventually turn many religious beliefs and practices on their head:

A passionate and unequivocal commitment to the idea that God is One with all creation. All faiths are but different paths to the One. The dignity of the female, establishing that men and women are equal. Rejection of the power or false status of the priesthood. Family life is supreme. True democracy, but not of the much-touted Greek or Roman variety which systemically excluded ninety percent of the populace, such as women, the workers, the poor and the slaves. A scripture in the vernacular. Literacy and education for the masses. The elevation of poetry and music by intertwining them with the Word. Express prohibition of tobacco and mind-altering substances. Public service at par with worship. The work ethic but primarily in the service of humanity ... and so on..

The revolution continues. We continue to be work in progress.

I am reminded as I look at each year's celebration of Hola Mohalla how detailed, meticulous and thorough our Gurus were in addressing the various aspects of our lives and demanding of us a complete rejection of the ills of old which were rooted in ignorance, exploitation, ritual and superstition, and replacing them with a modernity built on truth, integrity and enlightenment.

They created the ideal of the Renaissance Man and Woman, not in the limited European sense of the term but a template for everyman. The poor and the downtrodden, the uneducated and the menial labourer, all would have dibs on the good things of life, elbow to elbow, shoulder to shoulder, with the self-important and the self-appointed.

The festival of Hola Mohalla ("Hola") created by the Tenth Master is one such innovation which encapsules the spirit and letter of all that the Ten Gurus achieved in the preceding two-centuries and a half. To understand the Sikh

Hola, we need to understand Holi to which it was meant to be an antidote.

The Hindu festival of Holi has its basis in an ancient legend involving rivalry between deities in the Hindu firmament. The story goes that Hiranyakash, the king of demons, was as a result of his devotion to Brahma, one of the Hindu Trinity, elevated by the latter into a demi-god. However, the king's son Prahlad was a follower of Vishnu and refused to accept his father's suzerainty. Which led to a war between the competing gods.

The father king moves heaven and earth to kill his errant son who escapes with the help of his god. And so goes the story from atrocity to attempted murder to all-out-war, until the son is finally rescued by his father's sister Holika who holds the child in her lap and saves him from immolation while being burnt to cinders herself.

Incidentally, the metaphor of Prahlad's personal struggle against evil is oft used in Guru Granth Sahib as are many other stories from mythology.

Hence the day is celebrated in honour of Holika who had succumbed to her brother's cruelty. Other legends have been added through time to justify the revelry that has now come to be commonly associated with Holi, such as Krishna's playful stalking and teasing of the milkmaids. Somehow, the festival has also acquired sexual overtones and as anything else in India which has anything to do with inter-gender relationships, deteriorated into prurient practices.

There's no dearth of finely orchestrated and staged photo-ops every year when spectacular images appear in the media of merry-making amongst crowds of family and friends. No doubt pious religious ceremonies are held and healthy games played by families within households across the country. Some communities in the Hindi belt enact the war of the sexes literally by play-acting: women use sticks and batons to beat back their men-folk in mock-battles. Oddly these enactments mirror real-life drama being carried out in the streets and courthouses of every city, town and village in the country today.

Through sheer necessity the festival is properly observed mostly in the privacy of homes, behind closed doors and with the world shut out. For good reason. Because Holi across the length and breadth of the land has become a time for mischief and mayhem, for chaos and anarchy, a free-for-all during which anything goes. Which in India means no holds barred. A day – season, actually – dedicated to public violence, complete with religious licence.

It is not an Indian version of Guy Fawkes' Night or Halloween or the Mardi Gras. It is seen by the masses – the same hundreds of millions who have little food or education, and no sanitation – as a time to freely delve in country liquor and local brands of drugs and hallucinogens, be it ganja or toddy or contraband. The streets are taken over by goons and mobs who roam from neighbourhood to neighbour-hood looking for victims.

If you are male and get caught by a mob outdoors mere dabbing with coloured powders or a dunking in a tank of coloured water is not what's in the works. If there are open drains close by there's a good chance you will be dropped in them as is, no matter how unsanitary they are. A thrashing too could be in order if you are different, which could translate into being wealthy or better dressed or merely belonging to another faith.

If you are a female, pinching, pawing and groping by hungry hands will be the least of your problems. These are the days when incidents of rape and gang-rape go sky-high. Virtually no police reports are taken during these days of utter lawlessness, one of the reasons being that the police-men have taken the days off for the 'high-holiday' and are part of the street mobs.

It gets worse. I remember how each middle-class family would have to barricade itself behind closed doors and the relative safety of their homes, just in case a mob had any specific reason to target your home or your family. Wanting to tear down your doors was considered an innocent activity by drunks ... after all, it was Holi! There were instances when women were pulled out of their homes and brutalized in broad daylight while the men-folk were held back by the rest of the mob as spectators.

It is for these reasons that we as a family left town for a week or ten days every Holi season and came back only after receiving the clear that the 'religious festivities' were indeed over.

It is this specific context – it would have been no better in medieval India – that Guru Gobind Singh steered his Sikhs away from, and pointed them in the direction of a healthier and more civilized way of celebrating one's heritage. Hence, he marked the day after Holi – that is, after the Hindu mayhem had subsided – as Hola, the day when Sikhs would let their hair down.

Metaphorically, of course.

Imagine, a day created by a spiritual leader, an idea novel and unique in the history of world religions, for sports and physical prowess. Sikhs were to gather to compete in games and display their skills in horsemanship and weaponry, in weightlifting and wrestling, in athletics and even war games. All in the spirit of fair play and sportsmanship.

There would be a village fair and all that accompanies one. It would be held in the open and welcome both sexes, the sole object being to let each and every man, woman and child have fun. It is also a day free of religious observance. The feats and the acrobatics have no piety attached to them, nor are they dedicated to any petty god or goddess.

It is a day of fun, our Hola Mohalla ... good, clean, healthy fun. That's why we enjoy our Hindu friends and neighbours celebrating their day but reserve our own festivities for Hola.

THE COMB

Kangha. Comb. A small wooden artefact about two inches by three.

One of five articles of faith known as The Five K's or Kakkaars because each when written or uttered in Punjabi begins with the letter 'K'. It is worn on the person by Sikhs who choose to take on the full discipline of the faith.

It's the same simple, minimalist artefact which can still be bought today for a few cents, the innocuous object worn within the tresses of a Sikh's unshorn hair – rich or poor – almost like a hair accessory.

There's no dearth of public discussion and awareness about three of the Five K's. The Kesh (unshorn hair) and the Kirpan get lots of ink from Sikh and non-Sikh. The Karra (steel bracelet) is ever visible on a Sikh's right wrist and has acquired the aura of a fashion accessory, again, by both Sikh and non-Sikh.

The other two, the Kangha and the Kachhera (short breeches), being out of sight, remain mostly out of mind. Here I speak of the Kangha.

Like all things that hold symbolic value, the kangha too holds a whole world of significance and meaning. Unfortunately, we overlook all the nuances because it is the only one of the five Sikh articles of faith which has an obvious functional role in the routine of our everyday lives.

It's a comb. It sits tucked in beneath the hair-bun, the male joorrah or the female hair-do. It sees the light of day only when the hair needs to be re-groomed, the bun tightened or adjusted. And it is that role as a hair accessory that lends it its primary importance as a symbol.

Unshorn hair has long been central, at one stage or the other, to all communities and societies through human history. It embodied spirituality and a commitment to a higher purpose in life. Sikhism, however, took a marked departure from them all by recognizing it as something of beauty and value and therefore worth nurturing and celebrating.

Hinduism for example embraced renunciation as a path to salvation and extolled the denigration of the human body through neglect and self-punishment to achieve it. Disdain for the human body translated into neglect, resulting in matted, unclean, unkempt hair. It is a practice picked up by some other traditions, the most visible one in modern times being the Rastafarians.

Buddhists and Jains acknowledged hair as an integral part of the human form, but because they view human life as an affliction and a period of suffering, the uglification of the human body through shaving off its beauty became part of its route to salvation.

Jewish and Christian scriptures sing about the virtues of unshorn hair. Which then translated into its biblical role as a symbol of strength and beauty which could be wielded in war as a weapon or an instrument of punishment. Pagan and heathen practices quickly crept in as well through, inter alia, Greek and Roman mores and keeping or discarding hair became a fashion statement or an identity marker. Zoroastrians and Muslims too played with hair as a human appendage and carved rules around it, again, to express power, piety and wealth.

Sikhs, with their revolutionary idea that human life was a reward, not a punishment, sought to celebrate the human body. Unshorn hair therefore was to be valued, an idea which translated into the need to keep it clean and a sign of good health as opposed to neglecting it or sculpting it to fit into ever-changing political, social, cultural or religious world-views.

Hence, the kangha. A Sikh with unshorn hair is required by fiat to keep his tresses clean and healthy. Hence the daily *amrit-vela* (early morning) bath and the ever-present comb to keep the hair tangle-free. The requirement for unshorn hair was uniquely and intrinsically tied to cleanliness and a healthy lifestyle.

Just as the turban is to be unravelled and re-tied every morning (instead of being placed on the head like a cap or hat) in order to have it aired daily, so is the hair-bun to be undone every morning and evening and combed.

Parallel to the twin concept of *miri* and *piri* – the combination of spiritual and temporal obligations of every Sikh – is the principle that inner beauty is tied to physical health. Neither can be achieved without the other. The kangha therefore serves as a constant reminder of its role as a bridge between the two worlds which makes it as important as any of the other articles of our faith.

For me its significance doesn't stop there. If physical beauty, cleanliness and health are as important as their spiritual counterparts, then I believe it is incumbent on us as Sikhs to do all that is necessary to live balanced, healthy and aesthetic lives. It is for good reason that we visualize our Gurus as handsome figures who dressed well and lived well. Similarly we see our female Elders and heroes as beautiful and striking personalities.

We remember those who were subjected to torture or privation – Guru Arjan, Guru Tegh Bahadar, Mata Gujri, the Four Sahibzadas, to take but a few examples – not as victims but as triumphant, victorious and resplendent souls. In our mind's eye, they don't live as medieval, out-of-date historical personages, but as current, modern, ever-fresh sources of inspiration.

We don't require Guru Gobind Singh, the Tenth Master, to renounce the horse because popular lore describes Guru Nanak as walking from one land to another during his travels. Neither do we picture Guru Gobind Singh in long, floor-length *cholas* the way we do Guru Nanak, nor do we take the former to task for not imitating his predecessor in his physical appearance.

The kangha therefore represents modernity to me. It permits me, nay, requires me to be as well dressed as it is possible, in tune with the times to the extent my pocket allows me. If I can't afford an Armani, it doesn't mean I cannot walk around in simple, clean, ordinary clothes. There is no excuse in the world that justifies an uncouth or ungroomed appearance. One can have an unshorn beard, groomed or flowing, and a simple turban, and yet look as grand as a prince. One doesn't need to dress up like an eighteenth century nihang, even on Sundays, to celebrate one's Sikhi. One can be dressed in the latest fashions from Paris or more affordable outfits from Sears or Walmart. The female Punjabi attire, the *salwar-kameez*, is still my favourite, but I can see that they need not to be ill-fitting or unkempt to emphasize one's Punjabiness.

One's home too can be aesthetically pleasing without having a stick of furniture. Which means, the kangha reminds us, that the same attentiveness is due to the external, physical world as we give to our inner-selves. And vice-versa. The same applies to the work we do, to the seva we perform, the widgets we produce, the services we deliver, the families we rear, the friendships we nurture, the relationships we build ...

"Salvation is to be found," says Guru Arjan, "amidst play and laughter, adornment and nourishment, not away from it all ..." [GGS:522.10] Through active engagement, that is, not through neglect or renunciation.

That, in a nutshell, is the message I garner from the kangha-comb and I am reminded of it every day, not just on Sunday mornings or high-holidays.

VAISAKHI

I hadn't yet learnt how to handle deadlines well. This one, though I'd been given a wide berth – several months, I remember – had sneaked up on me and I'd started to sweat over it.

Barely into my teen years, I had a number of people goading me into writing. One of them was S. Mohan Singh Kalra, then the Editor of The *Sikh Review* in Calcutta. Having already published a few of my pieces, he had been encouraging me to write more often and to send him more.

I had at my father's insistence already done several write-ups for the two local English dailies, first on Guru Nanak, then on Guru Gobind Singh, and another a general piece on Sikhism. My published pieces in *The Sikh Review* until then had been in a similar vein.

This time around, I wanted to do something different. But I didn't know how or what. I tried several approaches but gave

173

up on them quickly and balls of crumpled manuscript pages began to pile up in my waste-paper basket. Finally I zeroed in on an idea, something I had never attempted before. Fiction! Not a bio, not a history, not an overview, but a story. It would have a historical core but it would allow me to weave my own tale and let my imagination wander into hitherto unexplored territory. I think I chose this route because it must have had the lure of appearing easier, something I could belt out in a couple of sittings since there would be, I thought, no boundaries.

Alas, I was in for a surprise.

Choosing a story-line was relatively easy. I had always been fascinated by the Vaisakhi story and the pure drama of the moment when young Guru Gobind Rai stood before the crowd of thousands on the hilltop in Anandpur on that fateful day in 1699, unsheathed his sword and stunned the audience with the strangest challenge they'd ever heard.

And I'd always been intrigued by the character of Daya Ram, the first one to answer the Guru's call: "Was anyone willing to offer his head for the sake of serving humanity?" So, I decided to do a fictional piece on the event, seen through Daya Ram's eyes. It would be narrated in his voice.

The story began with I, Daya Ram, making my way into Anandpur amidst a sea of fellow-travellers, all of them having responded to the clarion call to Sikhs from across the length and breadth of the land to gather for an audience before the Guru on the first day of the month of Vaisakh.

For a teenager yet to see much of the world I managed not too badly, taking Daya Ram through the last lap of his journey and delivering him into the sprawling scene of a bustling new city that had sprung up in answer to the summons. He and I, together, managed to finally get to the hilltop on the ominous morn.

I, Daya Ram, have managed to make my way to the front of the multitude, and am sitting there barely able to contain my excitement, chomping at the bit in anticipation. Any moment, I'm going to get to see, to have a *darshan*, of Guru Sahib. In the flesh.

And this is where I, the writer, got stalled.

For months I sit inside Daya Ram's head trying to fathom what is going on in his mind. His thoughts, his hopes, his aspirations, as the minutes and seconds unfold from that moment on. It takes me the better part of a year to live through the hours that follow, ultimately sweeping Daya Ram off his feet and into history.

Thus began my own journey of discovery.

I too, along with Daya Ram, get buffeted every which way, blown back and forth by winds that change course within split-seconds. We hear Gobind Rai's words and at the same time wince at the flash of the steel in his hand. It starts with exhilaration and awe. Then confusion. Fear. Faith. Skepticism. Love. Doubt. And self-doubt. Trust. Surrender. Indeed, it took me months as I sat there on the grass

175

before our Tenth Master struggling with questions of my own.

What would I have done if I had been there on that day in 1699? Would I have had the courage to stand up as Daya Ram did? Or would I have waited to see what happened to him? Would I have been one of the four that followed? Or would I have let Sahib and Dharam, Mohkam and Himmat go ahead, and held back to first see what happened next?

I remember how I let Daya Ram put up his hand, as I cringed in the shadows realizing there was no way I would have the courage to jump into the abyss. I came to the conclusion then, as I witnessed each of the Five step forward one by one and follow Him into the tent, that I could hold no candle to any of them. That there was no way in the world I could ever muster up what was needed, to do what they did.

If I learnt anything during that exercise it was that no ordinary metal and mettle are involved in forging nations. Today, half a century later, when I look back at my youthful dilemma I know that I still feel the way I did then.

You and I, we stand on the tall, firm, broad shoulders of The Five and therefore enjoy the ability to eye the horizon. For a teenager that I was when writing my fictional piece the toughest part of trying to get inside Daya Ram's head as he sat amongst the multitude on the First Vaisakhi was to figure out what would've gone through his mind then from one moment to the next.

Much of what Guru Gobind Rai said and did that morning is recorded in historical accounts; I had gained access to them all. But there was nothing available from Daya Ram's perspective. What was the impact of the Guru's words on the man? Daya Ram obviously knew they were life-transforming; after all, he himself was changed by them. But did he realize then the full ambit of the far-reaching revolution that was being enacted before his very eyes? How much did he know, what was the mental baggage he had brought with him, as he sat there bewildered by the sudden turn of events?

I was discovering not only a whole brave new world of fiction-writing – a struggle which continues to this day – but getting early glimpses into the miracle of Vaisakhi, nay, of Sikhi itself.

Through the successive decades as I have grown in years I have from time to time seated myself once again in that crowd. At first, each time, I am Daya Ram, and then he springs up, his head and hand held high. I tremble as I see him surge forward.

A coward, I stay behind, hiding in the sea of faces, all of us mesmerized sunflower-like by the same light. I hear Guru Gobind Rai's words. They are gentle words. Not of an overbearing, egotistical potentate. Not angry or dictatorial. But soft, like a lover's. He threatens no storms or pestilence. He demands no servitude. He claims no special familial link with God … just as a friend, a son, a bride, a lover. There is

177

no condescension, no looking down from above. No pretensions of I'd-rather-be-elsewhere-but-first-let-me-save-you.

He weaves no fantasies, creates no mutations of nature. He raises no mountains, parts no seas, shoots no nuclear thunder-bolts, unleashes no flying machines, brings no corpses alive, boasts no virgin births. He makes no promises of proxy, past, present or future. His life-trials are his alone, and will not release magic potions which will wash away your sins and mine.

There is no gimmickry. No lures, no marketing, no carrots, no sticks. No lies. All he says is: Stand up, push away your crutches and shed the cobwebs ... live a life of discipline ... clean ... healthy ... balanced ... steeped in humility ... grateful ... God-fearing ... sharing ... in service of others before self. Be a better person. Strong. Forever striving for excellence. Be fair and just. Fear no one, make no one fear you. Be compassionate.

I hear him and then I see him disappear into the tent. First with Daya Ram. Then, one after the other, with the four that followed. I know not what transpired behind the tent walls. He tells us nothing when he emerges each time. In his wisdom, it appears, there is nothing to tell.

He promises no conquests. Nor asks for any. Except that each one of us conquer ourselves personally. To transform ourselves. To live lives of dignity, to value our own rights and freedoms and those of others.

And in doing so pray our own prayers, fight our own fights, labour and strive for the betterment of ourselves and of others.

Miracles. What miracles, he asks? If you want miracles, he says, go forth and perform your own miracles. No one, no one, he reiterates, is capable of performing your miracles. You can't buy them, you can't steal them, you cannot borrow them, you can't transfer them. Everyone can and must, he says, work his own miracles. Live life to the fullest, and each one of you will be as powerful as a legion. The world will be yours but not until you have learnt to rule over yourself.

This is where I get stuck in the writing of my story.

This ... here ... what happened on the hill-top, is the story. All that I know of it so far. Once I get here, I can't get beyond it. I see nothing else.

Is there more?

IS GOD DEAD? OR IS HE ALIVE?

A massive new multi-billion dollar industry has sprung up around God and it is taking the world by storm. Actually, the term 'billion-dollar' doesn't mean much any more given the infinite capacity of the super greedy and the unscrupulous to devour anything that isn't bolted down – or is.

The God industry.

I'm not talking about religion. I'm talking about the selling of two slogans both equally inane and meaningless, the willing surrender of millions of souls in every faith system known to man today, and their being sucked into the gargantuan marketing vortex around their jingoism.

One side claims "God is dead". The other that "God is alive." And there is a third group in the middle milking it with equal fervour, claiming to offer an objective dialogue between the two. The silliness isn't anything new. It's been going on since time immemorial with 'philosophers' gazing interminably at their navels and then sharing their lint-pickings with the world.

I remember being urged as a teenager to read Bertrand Russell's *Why I Am Not A Christian*, followed by the endless meanderings of Krishnamurti. I am glad I gave in and read them all. They were written well and were addictive for a young and hungering mind. But it didn't take long for me to realize that they were nothing but mind-games built on premises which were as weak as any house of cards. Fun to read and a good way to kill time but adding little to the big questions that begin to haunt us as we make our way on our life-journey.

Though increasingly aware of the vacuity and their fatuity, I continued to read others that came my way. Why? Because some of them were necessary reading if one was to remain abreast of the current lingo. Others were cultish and needed to be understood before you could intelligently reject them.

So I dug through the likes of G.K. Chesterton and C.S. Lewis. And, of course, Lobsang Rampa and Carlos Castaneda and various permutations and combinations thereof. Mercifully, they were few and far between.

But now, it's turned out to be an all-out war. There's the 'God Delusion' crowd, and there're the 'God Is Alive And

Well' crusaders. At each others throats as if the outcome will determine the future of humanity or civilization as we know it. And like all wars, it is fuelled by greed and profit hiding under the skirts of dogma and ideology.

There are books and films, both feature and documentary, and TV shows and serials coming out of our ears. The so-called social media is afire with anti-social rhetoric, and fervour and immorality hitherto reserved for religious and proselytizing nuts. Confusion reigns. The side rooting for God has membership in all religions and they all claim they are enemies of what they call, deceivingly, secularization. But they get schizophrenic not knowing when to fight for God and when to switch to fighting for their own 'god'. They know in their hearts that if they win the argument for God, their own diminished 'god' loses out. It's a game of thrust and parry and a lot of blood is spilt in the process. No matter that much of the injury is self-inflicted.

Then there are the atheists and the agnostics who, encouraged by the new wind in their sails, have themselves become crusaders and are poised to start an Inquisition of their own. Gone is the timidity that usually comes with doubt and uncertainty, hitherto, the very strengths of this lot.

Women, gays, and minorities, though still smarting from the slings and arrows of the smug majority, they too have jumped into the fray and are not interested in taking prisoners.

I've tired of these games. I have no patience left for fools of either ilk, the pro-God and the anti-God. I have no time to read any of their drivel any more. Been there, done that and there's nothing left worth writing home about.

The other day I got pushed into viewing two recent film offerings. Both came with high praise. I had an evening free, so I gave them a shot.

The first, *God is Not Dead* proved to be utter piffle. I gave it 40 minutes and then pulled out the DVD, angry at myself for having dropped my guard and allowed it to waste my time.

The second one, *The Sunset Limited*, looked more promising only because it starred Samuel L. Jackson and Tommy Lee Jones; I admire their work. Didn't last more than half-an-hour with this one. It was a dialogue building towards a debate between one arguing for pro, the other for con.

I can't take it any more. I'm just not interested anymore in other people's mental gymnastics around the 'god' they have created in their own, respective images. I am sixty-nine years old now and if I don't know by now that, a) it's a personal and lonely journey, looking for an answer; and b) no matter who says it, no matter what anyone says, it's at best a wild guess and almost guaranteed to be wrong. If I don't know this by now, well, then I've wasted my life, haven't I?

So, I'm not going down that road with anyone else any more. I'd rather read *Harry Potter* and watch *Star Trek* than dive into the flotsam and jetsam of busybodies who know nothing but have discovered that their mental doodles sell and that there are a lot of gulls out there to make them rich in the process.

I know I don't have the answers but I am content with that and am comfortable with merely looking at the sunrise and smelling the flowers. I do know one thing though. That God isn't Jabba The Hutt who is sitting somewhere in a celestial nightclub sending fire and brimstone and locusts and plagues our way. He isn't a multi-armed or hydra-headed half-monster. He isn't a Houdini, he doesn't do tricks, he doesn't bend the rules of life and death merely because it makes great poetry.

Chances are, He isn't even a He. Or a She. Or an It. Or Them.

I have found meaning in my life. I've seen a pattern, I recognize a design. And I'm grateful for that. The rest, with grace, will or will not follow. I'm fine with that. The little bit that I know or I think I know, given my limited faculties, is enough. Beyond that I don't really care if your God is dead or alive or was never born or is reborn or is going to come back one fine, dreadful day. Those of you who wish to drag me into one more dialogue or discussion or theory or whatever, all I have to say is: Get a life! Go grab a cup of java, step out into the sun, stand on the deck, listen to the birds.

Or take a prozac. Get a job. Find a lover. Do something, anything, which gives you joy.

Live!

For heaven's sake.

BEING DIFFERENT

I recall one evening when after a particularly busy day I was able to take some much-needed time-off. No computer, no e-mails. No television. No breaking news. No telephone. With all of them switched off it didn't take me long to unwind. I relax easily when free of the amenities of 'convenience' with which life has had us all tied-up. Stillness, that precious commodity today, is so essential to charge our batteries. This was an evening of stillness.

After dinner I turned to the one thing that helps me instantly transport myself to another world and drive away at least for a few hours all the goings on in the world: a good movie. I pored over my 'new-and-never-seen-before' shelf of DVDs and picked one at random. Seemed like a good one; it featured a favourite actor, Kristin Scott Thomas.

It turned out to be captivating. A good story, well-produced, though heavy. But it did the trick: it kept my mind off things.

It was a film about the Jewish Holocaust. With a twist. The scene was set in France in Gay Paree. The perpetrators? Not the Germans, but the French: a well-suppressed fact of history.

There too, Jews – men, women and children – had been required to identify themselves with a large patch of the Star of David affixed prominently atop each layer of clothing. The Yellow Star it came to be known as, always inscribed with the word "Jude" on it (German for a "Jew"). So that each Jew could be instantly identified by the populace as such.

One day suddenly military trucks arrived in their neighbourhoods, herded them off to trains and thereon to concentration camps and to the darkest depths of Nazi ignominy, their mass murder. There's more to the plot of the film, but this was the general backdrop.

Last night the highlights of the story occupied my dreams. I have the good fortune of always being able to sleep as if I'm 'done', having 'sold all of my camels at the market'. But still, my dreams work as crucibles where my writing simmers and cooks in my subconscious and takes shape. I wake up in the morning, sometimes with the germ of an idea, sometimes a new line of thought; sometimes even a well-baked story, complete with opening and closing lines, with only the middle missing.

I woke up this morning thinking about the Yellow Star. Is there a difference between the Yellow Star and the turban I wear, I wondered. I've been pondering over this all morning.

Some interesting similarities. Both identify the wearer instantly as belonging to a specific religious group. Each is eye-catching. Unambiguous. Stands out. Proclaims. Allows no escape.

But some significant differences separate them.

One is an externally imposed instrument of oppression, the other a voluntary self-expression of personal sovereignty. One hopefully, mercifully, never to be used again ever in the manner in which the Nazis did. The other, always to be worn with regal pride, like a crown.

The Star of David for many Jews has mystical connotations. The Nazis distorted it and used it nefariously. I don't subscribe to any mystical connotations, however, to the turban. Some people do go airy-fairy, new-age style, and claim it protects the 'third-eye' or the 'tenth door', picking up metaphors from scripture and literalizing them.

Balderdash, all of it. There's nothing mystical about the turban. I wear it for the most worldly of reasons. I've worn it all of my adult life. I wear it all the time I'm in public and much of the time I'm at home. It is part of me. It is part of my self-image. And of how others see me and know me. I can't imagine ever not wearing it. So much so that I forget I'm wearing it. Now and then I even get a bit of a shock when I walk past a mirror in a public place and catch a glimpse of my reflection; the shock that I look different. Surrounded by those who look different, I forget that I look different from them.

'Different' is the operative word. Different, not in an "us" and "them" way, but in that we are all unique and special and celebrate it. Different not by accident, but by design.

I don't know of a single human being – and I've met more than my fair share in my lifetime – who doesn't spend some time every day primping and preening before a mirror with only one goal in mind: to look different. Do you know of anyone, even a single person, who spends his/her fashion time, money and sensibilities, in trying to look exactly the same as the rest of the world?

So the turban simply makes it more obvious that I am indeed different. Because I am. The reason why I wear a turban is to be clearly identified as a Sikh. Period.

I have a bundle of beliefs, like everyone else. And I stand behind them through thick and thin. They wouldn't be worth much, would they, if I denied them or hid them or pretended I didn't have them, if and when the going got tough. I want my friends to know what I stand for and I want my detractors to know what I stand for. Not to foist my beliefs on them but to tell them that I respect them for their beliefs and I expect to be respected for mine.

Try sending your opinion as a Letter to the Editor to any respectable journal, any newspaper worth its mettle, and insist on anonymity and see where it gets you. Because your opinions and beliefs are worth nothing if you're not willing to stand behind them and bear the consequences.

Try being a witness, or a plaintiff, or a defendant, or a judge, prosecutor or defence counsel in a court of law and say you don't want to disclose who you are and see how far it'll get you. It's the same principle behind the Sikh turban.

Even when a madman steps in front of me, gun in hand, I want him to know that I'm a Sikh if that's what he wants to know. Let the chips fall where they may. Did anyone think that a turban is a fashion accessory? Or something that you wear if and only when you're amongst friends?

Half of the Hindus on the Indian subcontinent became Muslim when the Mughals terrorized the populace over the course of several centuries. It wouldn't have happened if they had stood behind their beliefs, willing to pay a price if necessary. The other half that was left proceeded to shed its Hindu articles of faith and even hid many of its practices at the first confrontation with 'modernity'. Today, there isn't much of real Hinduism left simply because no one is willing to pay the price of holding principled convictions.

If you're not willing to stand behind what you purport are your beliefs they're not worth writing home about. It's easy today, in India for example, to hide your faith when it is expedient to do so. Try finding those who profess any faith and actually practice it. Similarly it has become easy everywhere in the world to hide your faith, any conviction, as soon as it becomes inconvenient to be identified by it.

Some conviction, that.

But if you are a Sikh and mean it, it is a basic requirement that you don't allow yourself the luxury of turning into a coward when it is profitable or beneficial not to be identified as such. Sure, that means that Sikhi isn't meant for every one. Nothing wrong with that. Each of us has a role to play in life and every role has value and deserves respect. Being a Sikh is not better, it's not worse. But let's be clear: that's what being a Sikh entails. That is one of the things that makes you a Sikh: standing out, out-standing. Niraala, Nyaara.

That's why Sikhs are known as protectors of the weak and the needy, the oppressed and the voiceless, wherever Sikhs live, wherever they go. For one basic reason – because they can't change their colours when the going gets tough. You can frown and scowl, you can fret and sulk, you can discriminate and you can persecute, or you can walk in with a gun into my place of worship, rest assured I'll be there ... always with my turban.

So that you'll know that I am, for better or worse, a Sikh.

THE REFEREE

Been watching the World Cup soccer games? Gripping, aren't they?

I can see why it captivates so many around the world to distraction. The passion and the fervour are often so intense that emotions translate into riots and mayhem. There's no other game that consumes us so universally from across the oceans and continents, cutting a swathe through languages, nationalities and ethnicities.

What is it about it that beggars all of its competitors in comparison, be it cricket, or hockey (field or ice), basketball, baseball, golf ... whatever?

The raw exhibition of muscle and sinew, coupled with a chess-like battle of wits? Also, there are no implements to give one a false extension: no bats or sticks or clubs. No masks or helmets or cages to save one from the clash of brain and brawn with matching brain and brawn.

One of the things that may be the most appealing is that it is open to the average human being. You don't need to be a giant seven feet tall to gain advantage over your adversary. Or a midget to make you more nimble and swift. Or rich and privileged to be able to afford state-of-the-art paraphernalia and gain access onto the playing field.

All this and more I discovered about soccer – football, it was called then – in my younger days though I never showed much promise on the field. I even tried a stint as goalkeeper and quickly realized, my coaches and I in tandem, that the game deserved better.

Now I enjoy the game all the more in its World Cup manifestation every four years, thanks to the marvel of live television. For God's sake, we get a better view of the action than even the players on the field. Our vision zooms in and out at will, hovers over and then dives fearlessly into the melee. It soars with the ball, and then, if need be, we get a Tiepolo-like shot from below as it spins back to earth.

But if the players dazzle us with their gladiatorial skills what impresses me all the more is the extraordinary role played by The Referee.

To avoid any confusion let me first make something perfectly clear. Here, I'm not referring to the poor lone soul left adrift and unprotected in the midst of the twenty-two charging bulls, armed with a whistle, a spray can (should

194

be pepper spray, but it is only chalk) and a pack of coloured cards. The one who flits back and forth, his first job being to avoid being kicked in the shins or buried in a stampede, and secondly to umpire between the multiple and simultaneous goings-on at any given moment of the ninety minutes of the game over a sprawl of land almost two acres in size. That is, more than 86,000 square feet. All the while, of course, with a hundred thousand banshees screaming from the stands in judgement of his every ruling over the shenanigans of the players that surround him.

Don't get me wrong. I don't mean to belittle his task, or of those of his assistants who have the better sense and foresight to stand safely at a distance, demarcated by a line that the players cannot cross. They're all good men and women, brave and wise, and perform their roles well enough to deserve a Cup of their own.

But by 'The Referee', I of course refer to a greater authority who has the ultimate say in all that happens on the soccer field. He determines who wins, who loses and, worst of all, who gets sent to the purgatory of a tie. In front of The Referee, all others, whether FIFA trained and approved and appointed or not, pale into insignificance. He's not even answerable to FIFA, the all-powerful, all-pervasive, ever-present Fédération Internationale de Football Association.

In fact, I dare to suggest, FIFA itself is answerable to The Referee. What do I base this extraordinary and seemingly outlandish statement on? Surely you too have seen the evidence? Everyone who enters the arena knows this and acknowledges this fact not just upon entering or leaving but also at frequent intervals. The spectators too, of course. The coaches and the managers, even the water-boys. The lowly referees, assistants and all.

And the players. O, especially the players. You can see it even as the players emerge from the tunnel into the sunlight. Their lips are moving silently. In prayer. As the sun rays fall on their faces their eyes are raised skywards in quick, split-second supplication. Some join their hands, others put their joined index fingers to their lips after doing the sign of the cross. Others bow to the ground and touch it with their finger-tips, and then bless themselves with a touch of the same hallowed hands to their foreheads.

Christian and Muslim and Jew or whatever, with talismans and shibboleths galore, they bow and pay homage to The Great Referee in the sky. Every favourable ruling, every advance against the enemy, every goal, every victory, is punctuated with an obeisance.

If mere sincerity and intensity were to be the criteria, The Referee would readily grant each of them a goal. But He can't. Just as He cannot make both sides win in a war even if both claim His sponsorship. The Referee is a tough cookie. He is not swayed by all the times a whistle goes in a player's favour and he, the player, subtly points his index fingers up, or rolls his eyes heavenwards. Or whispers loving *bon mots*. Or kisses his fingers in His proxy.

He can clearly see the thespian pleas of each player as he tumbles, but unlike the earthly umpire, He doesn't have to decide whether the spill was real or fake, whether the push was accidental or contrived, whether the moans and groans are from injury or disappointment. And whether there is someone to be blamed and if so, who. He doles out no penalties, no corner shots. He flashes no yellow cards. He's amenable to no flattery. No bribes or threats. No negotiations or deals. He is oblivious to all.

Just as foolish wars are won by one and then the other, so are these games won by one, then the other. Not by dint of their religious affliation, but despite it. For a while each gets his fifteen minutes of Andy Warhol fame, and is allowed to claim supremacy and then is relegated once again to the existential sidelines.

After all, they are called G-A-M-E-S.

I don't think the soccer players, no matter of which religious ilk, have yet realized that on the play-field sharpness both mental and physical is all that counts. Concentrate on playing the game, not looking for outside assistance. It's how you play that matters. And it's the play itself that matters, not its collateral benefits, the money it brings or the accolades it generates.

Like everything in life, I think, The Big Referee plays along with us by merely throwing the dice and lets the chips fall where they may. The rest, whether we reap any personal and lasting benefits, is up to us. And in that, there is no race, no competition. Each one of us is on his or her own.

That, I gather, is the only rule of the game imposed by The Referee.

ACKNOWLEDGMENTS

Everything good in my life has come to me through my late father, Sardar Ishar Singh and mother, Sardarni Mahinder Kaur. If you like anything in this book, it is all part of their legacy; the rest is entirely mine and mine alone to blame.

The very existence of this book I owe to my grandchildren. They have inspired me, their Nana, to create a record of their maternal heritage before it gets too late ... I have just turned 69!

My daughter Gehna Kaur Singh-Kareckas has been a life-long editor, sometimes the first, at other times the last one to review my writings before they go for publication. I have also enjoyed precious feedback from my son-in-law Andrew Singh-Kareckas who has graciously assumed a similar role.

Some dear friends deserve mention: Carol Klein has given me priceless feedback. Haroon Siddiqui too, through the years, has helped shape my writing. Tony Leighton's insights and ability to reduce things to their quintessence have been invaluable. My youngest sister Sartaj Kaur's feedback too has proved indispensable.

Birinder Singh Ahluwalia I have already mentioned in the dedication of this book as one who has been the strength behind my writing for decades. Bicky Singh of SikhLens, Los Angeles has been a stalwart in helping with the production of this book. Details from master sword-maker Jot Singh Khalsa's exquisitely crafted Khalsa Kirpans adorn the front and back covers of this book. Andrew Hydon did his magic on the keyboard to help me organize the manuscript.

My muse throughout the gestation and birth of this book has been my love and partner, Marketa Holtebrinck. I have relied heavily on her constructive criticism on every aspect of this book. Without her support, it would have been an insurmountable struggle.

To all of the above and many more who have escaped mention through the sieve of my faltering memory but are embedded in my heart, I am indebted beyond measure.

Finally, many of the pieces that appear in this book have earlier seen the light of day in one form or the other in *The Toronto Star*, *The Huffington Post*, *The Kitchener-Waterloo Record*, *The Guelph Mercury* and, of course, the online magazine, *sikhchic.com*.

GLOSSARY

Akal Takht – seat of temporal Sikh authority. Symbolically it stands across the causeway from the Golden Temple in Amritsar which constitutes the spiritual heart of the Sikhs.

Akhand Paatth – non-stop reading of the Guru Granth cover to cover. It usually takes about 48 hours.

Amrit – literally, ambrosial nectar. It is the name given to the ceremony that initiates a Sikh into the Khalsa.

Amritdhari – a Sikh, male or female, who has taken the Amrit initiation and the vows of the Khalsa.

Amrit Vela – literally, the ambrosial hour. Early morning, around or before sunrise.

Anand Kaaraj – Sikh wedding ceremony.

Baata – large steel bowl used for the Amrit ceremony. Smaller versions are also to be found in Punjabi kitchens.

Baba – grand old man; an honorific used for older or venerable men.

Bandhi Chhor – Sikh festival that coincides with Diwali.

Baani – verses from Sikh scripture.

Beta – literally, son. Term of endearment used for a child, son or daughter.

Bhai – literally, brother; an honorific.

Bhangra – Punjabi harvest dance. Now also identified with an associated music genre.

Bhen ji – literally, elder sister

Bibi – honorific used for women. Lady, mother.

Biji – abbreviation of 'Bibi ji'. Mother, grandmother.

Bir Aasan – The warrior's pose; a sitting position which allows one to spring to action instantly. Required of initiates during the Amrit ceremony.

Chaali Muktey – the Forty Liberated Ones – soldier-martyrs from Guru Gobind Singh's army.

Chhaba – a dome-shaped tasseled ornament, usually made of gold or silver, hung as an adornment from the canopy above the Guru Granth Sahib.

Chhabeel – tent, shack, vending hut.

Chandova – ornamental canopy above the Guru Granth Sahib to convey the regality of the Living Guru's presence.

Chardi Kalaa – Sikh concept of eternal optimism.

Chaur Sahib – fly whisk used over the Guru Granth Sahib to convey regality.

Chief Khalsa Diwan – Sikh institution overseeing Sikh affairs.

Chola – long, loose shirt.

Daal – lentil dish, staple of meals served in a Gurdwara langar.

Darbar Sahib – popularly known as The Golden Temple in Amritsar. Also called Harmandar Sahib.

Darshan – having audience with a personage; vision. Usually used by Sikhs in a spiritual context, e.g., vis-à-vis Guru or God.

Dasam Granth – Book of The Tenth Guru, containing his writings and those of the 52 poets in his Court.

Dastaar – turban.

Dastaar Sajaani – ceremony around the inaugural donning of the turban.

Degh – literally, pot. Utensil used in preparation of langar. Term is also used metaphorically for the Sikh's duty to feed the poor and hungry.

Desi – literally, from the countryside. Term used for Indians in general.

Devi – Hindu goddess, idol.

Devta – Hindu male deity, idol.

Diwali – festival of lights.

Five K's, or Kakkaar – the five articles of faith of the Khalsa.

Gatka – Sikh martial arts.

Ghuggni – Black gram lentil dish, native to Bihar. Eaten as snack or in curry form.

Golden Temple – Sikh spiritual centre in Amritsar, Punjab.

Gulab Jal – rose flavoured water

Gurbani – Sikh scripture. Literally, the compositions of the Gurus. Verses contained in the Guru Granth Sahib.

Gurdwara – Sikh place of worship.

Gurmukhi – the script used most commonly by Sikhs to write Punjabi; the script of the Guru Granth Sahib. The Shahmukhi script is used by Pakistani-Punjabis.

Guru – honorific used for the founders of the Sikh Faith and its Scripture.

Guru Granth Sahib – Sikh Scripture. Regarded as The Living Word.

Gurupurab – High holiday associated with any of the Gurus.

Gut – French-braid like hair arrangement traditionally used for young Sikh boys. Not common any more. Pronounced as in 'put' but with a soft 't'.

Gutka – Sikh prayer book containing the daily liturgy, usually five compositions known as the *Punj Baanis*. Pronounced as in 'put'.

Harmandar – literally, the House of God; the central shrine of the Golden Temple

Hindu – religion of the majority in India. Sikhs, distinctly different in beliefs, constitute a mere 2 to 3 % of the population.

Hindutva – an extreme Hindu fundamentalist ideology riddled by violence and intolerance.

Hola Mohalla – Sikh annual festival of sports.

Holi – featival of colours.

Hukam – a passage selected at random from the Guru Granth Sahib, the Sikh Scripture, as a daily inspiration.

Jaap Sahib – a composition by Guru Gobind Singh. Part of a Sikh's daily liturgy.

Jaloos – parade, procession.

Jathaa – group.

Jathedar – literally, headman or leader. Term is used for senior administrator of a Sikh institution.

Jee-o – respectful 'yes'. Also used as a term of endearment.

Ji – honorific denoting respect, deference and reverence. Also used as a respectful 'yes'.

Joorrah – hair bun. Used for both males and females.

Kaar Seva – volunteer service, usually referring to projects around the construction or refurbishing of a gurdwara.

Kacchi Lassi – Punjabi cold drink made of milk, rose-water, cardamom.

Kachhera – short breeches. One of the Five K articles of faith.

Kakkaars – Sikh articles of faith.

Kanga – small comb. One of the Five K articles of faith.

Karra – steel bracelet. One of the Five K articles of faith.

Karraah Prashad – sweet pudding served as sacrament after a Sikh prayer service. Made of flour, sugar, butter.

Kathaa – exegesis; explanation of a verse or concept from the Sikh scripture.

Kaur – Princess. The common last name given to Sikh females.

Kavi Darbar – poetry night.

Kesh – unshorn hair. One of the Five K articles of faith.

Khalistan – the name given by some Sikhs to the aspiration of an independent Sikh homeland.

Khalsa – a Sikh Order dedicated to a life of spiritual discipline and public service.

Kirat Karni – work ethic. One branch of a three-pronged Sikh motto.

Kirpan – a knife or sword. One of the Five K articles of faith.

Kirtan – singing of verses from Guru Granth Sahib.

Kirtaniya – one who does kirtan.

Komagata Maru – the ship of Sikh immigrants that arrived in Vancouver harbour in 1914.

Langar – the Sikh institution of a free kitchen run by volunteers, an integral part of every gurdwara. Also refers to the food served there.

Looh – literally, furnace. The height of the summer season on the Subcontinent.

Mandir – Hindu temple.

Maasi – mother's sister, aunt.

Mata – literally, mother. An honorific used for senior or venerable women.

Miri – worldly matters or obligations.

Mitthhaaee – Punjabi home-made sweets.

Morcha – political struggle.

Mughals – a ruling dynasty which enforced Islam on the Subcontinent for several centuries.

Naam Juppna – prayer, meditative worship. One branch of a three-pronged Sikh motto.

Nihang – member of a historical Sikh unit of warriors renowned for their valour.

Niraala – extraordinary.

Nitnem – daily Sikh prayers; liturgy.

Nyaara – standing out, exceptional.

Paatth – recitation or reading of scriptural verses.

Pakhand – hypocrisy.

Palki – throne used for the Guru Granth Sahib.

Panth – nation.

Parbhaat Pheri – pre-dawn group of singers doing the rounds in a neighbourhood singing festive hymns, similar to carol-singing in the West.

Parkaash – presence. Literally, light.

Parshaad – sacrament. Literally, grace.

Patka – under-turban used by Sikh children or youth engaged in sports.

Piri – Spiritual matters or obligations.

Puggri – turban.

Punjabi – the language of Punjab. Language of the Sikhs and several other communities. Now spoken around the world in the diaspora.

Punjabi Suba – Punjabi-speaking State.

Punj Pyarey – the Five Beloved Ones. The first five members of the Khalsa. The five who administer the Amrit during the Khalsa initiation ceremony.

Raag – musical arrangements in Sikh classical music.

Raagi – a minstrel who sings verses from the Guru Granth, accompanied by musical instruments. Usually, but not necessarily, in groups of three.

Raj – literally, rule. Often used for the British Empire ('British Raj').

Raja – male ruler.

Rani – female ruler or a Raja's consort.

208

Rumala – the regal raiments in which the Guru Granth Sahib is adorned.

Saafa – turban.

Sahib – honorific used for an elder, a guest, Guru and God. Also added to religious icons.

Saccha Padshah – the True King. Term used for the Gurus.

Saccha Sauda – literally, the True Bargain. Refers to a historical and seminal incident from Guru Nanak's childhood.

Sahibzada – son, prince. Honorific used for Guru Gobind Singh's sons all four of whom were martyred.

Salwar-Kameez – the shirt-and-trouser tunic traditionally worn by Punjabi women.

Sangat – congregation.

Sant – a saintly person. A title unfortunately also misused by many today by charlatans posing as 'god-men'.

Sant-Sipahi – Saint-Soldier.

Sarbat da bhalla – the closing words of the daily Sikh prayer (*Ardaas*). For the welfare of all humanity.

Sardar – the honorific used for all Sikh males instead of Mr., Monsieur, Shri, etc. Literally, chieftain.

Sardarni – the honorific used for all Sikh females instead of Mrs, Ms, Miss, Shrimati, Madame, Mademoiselle, etc.

Satnaam – literally, the True Name. Used for God in the Sikh scripture.

Sat Sri Akaal – Sikh greeting: God (the Timeless One) is Truth.

Savaa Lakh – literally, 125,000. Refers to every Sikh's aspiration to be as effective as a legion.

Seva – selfless volunteer service.

Sevadaar – one who performs Seva.

Shabad – literally, the Word. Hymn, verse from Sikh scripture.

Shabaash – pat on the back in approval, encouragement.

Sher-di-bacchi – literally, Sher's daughter. In common Punjabi parlance: the progeny of a lion.

Sikh – one who practices the Sikh Faith.

Sikhi – Sikhism; teachings of the Sikh Gurus.

Singh – the common name given to all Sikh males.

Siri Sahib – Sikh name for God. Also, for the full-sized kirpan.

Sri – honorific used for the Gurus and God.

Tabla – a pair of drums played in accompaniment to the singing of Sikh hymns.

Takht – one of five seats of Sikh administrative authority.

Turban – the head-covering worn by Sikh males and some females.

Vaisakh – a month in the Punjabi calendar roughly coinciding with April-May.

Vaisakhi – the festival and high holiday associated with the formation of the Khalsa on the 1st of Vaisakh (April 13), 1699.

Waheguru – the Sikh/Punjabi term for The One, God of all creation.

Wund Chhakna – literally, share and eat. The practice of charity, one branch of a three-pronged Sikh motto.

THE AUTHOR

Tapishar 'Sher' Singh has had multiple careers: author, lecturer, litigation lawyer, police commissioner, editor, publisher, and journalist, including stints as a national current-affairs columnist, travel writer, television host and radio commentator. He is also the founder of the online magazine *sikhchic.com*, *The Spinning Wheel Film Festival*, the annual *Guelph Lecture On Being Canadian*, and Toronto's annual *Vaisakhi Gala*. He now resides in Mount Forest, a village in rural Ontario, Canada.

Sher welcomes feedback on the book: TSherSingh@GMail.com